RELATED TITLES FOR COLLEGE-BOUND STUDENTS

Titles for the New SAT starting March 12, 2005

The NEW SAT

The NEW SAT with CD-ROM

The NEW SAT Critical Reading Workbook

The NEW SAT Writing Workbook

Vocabulary-Building for the SAT

Extreme SAT Vocabulary Flashcards Flip-O-Matic

SAT Vocab Velocity

Frankenstein: A Kaplan SAT Score-Raising Classic

The Ring of McAllister: A Score-Raising Mystery
Featuring 1,046 Must-Know SAT Vocabulary Words

PSAT

The NEW PSAT

KAPLAN

Test Prep and Admissions

SAT

Vocabulary Flashcards

Flip-O-Matic

Second Edition

By the Staff of Kaplan, Inc.

Simon & Schuster

NEW YORK · LONDON · SYDNEY · TORONTO

Kaplan Publishing
Published by Simon & Schuster
1230 Avenue of the Americas
New York, NY 10020

Contributing Editors: Seppy Basili and Jon Zeitlin
Executive Editor: Jennifer Farthing
Production Manager: Michael Shevlin
Project Editor: Sandy Gade

October 2004
10 9 8 7 6 5 4 3 2 1
Manufactured in the United States of America
Published simultaneously in Canada

ISBN 0-7432-6427-4

HOW TO USE THIS BOOK

Kaplan's fantastic *SAT Vocabulary Flashcards Flip-O-Matic, Second Edition* is perfectly designed to help you learn 500 essential SAT vocabulary words in a quick, easy, and fun way. Simply read the vocabulary word (including part of speech and pronunciation) on the front of the flashcard and then flip to the back to see its definition, an example sentence with the SAT word in action, and synonyms of the word. Once you've mastered a particular word, clip or fold back the corner of the flashcard so that you can zip right by it on your next pass through the book. The *Flip-O-Matic* is packed with vocabulary—remember to flip the book over and flip through the other half! As a special bonus, we've included an SAT word root list at the back of this book for extra studying power. Grouping words together that share a common root meaning is a terrific and efficient way to familiarize yourself with strange or tough words you may encounter on the test.

Looking for still more SAT prep? Be sure to pick up a copy of Kaplan's comprehensive *SAT 2005 with CD-ROM*, complete with full-length practice tests

Good luck, and happy flipping!

ABASE

verb (uh <u>bays</u>)

someone passionately devoted to a cause

The *zealot* had no time for those who failed to share his strongly held beliefs.

Synonyms: enthusiast; fanatic; militant; radical

to humble; to disgrace

After his immature behavior, John *abased* himself in my eyes.

Synonyms: demean; humiliate

ZEALOT

noun (zeh luht)

ABDICATE

verb (aab duh kayt)

to join together

As soon as the farmer had *yoked* his oxen together, he began to plow the fields.

Synonyms: bind; harness; pair

to give up a position, right, or power

> With the angry mob clamoring outside the palace, the king *abdicated* his throne and fled.

Synonyms: cede; quit; relinquish; resign; yield

YOKE

verb (yohk)

ABERRATION

noun (aa buhr ay shuhn)

fear or hatred of foreigners or strangers

Countries in which *xenophobia* is prevalent often have more restrictive immigration policies than countries which are more accepting of foreign influences.

Synonyms: bigotry; chauvinism; prejudice

something different from the usual

> Due to the bizarre *aberrations* in the author's behavior, her publicist decided that the less the public saw of her, the better.

Synonyms: abnormality; anomaly; deviation; irregularity

XENOPHOBIA

noun (zee noh foh bee uh)

ABEYANCE

noun (uh <u>bay</u> uhns)

withered, shriveled, wrinkled

The *wizened* old man was told that the plastic surgery necessary to make him look young again would cost more money than he could imagine.

Synonyms: atrophied; desiccated; gnarled; mummified; wasted

temporary suppression or suspension

> Michelle held her excitement in *abeyance* while the college review board considered her application.

Synonyms: deferral; delay; dormancy; postponement; remission

WIZENED

adj (wih zuhnd)

ABJECT

adj (<u>aab</u> jehkt)

playful, fanciful

The ballet was *whimsical*, delighting the children with its imaginative characters and unpredictable sets.

Synonyms: capricious; chameleonic; erratic; fickle; mutable

miserable, pitiful

When we found the *abject* creature lying on the ground, we took it inside and tended to its broken leg.

Synonyms: lamentable; pathetic; sorry

WHIMSICAL

adj (wihm sih cuhl)

ABSTRUSE

adj (<u>aab</u> stroos) (<u>uhb</u> stroos)

to sharpen; to stimulate

The delicious odors wafting from the kitchen *whet* Jack's appetite, and he couldn't wait to eat.

Synonyms: hone; grind; strop

difficult to comprehend

> The philosopher's elucidation was so clear that he turned an *abstruse* subject into one his audience could grasp.

Synonyms: complex; esosteric; profound

WHET

verb (weht)

ACERBIC

adj (uh <u>suhr</u> bihk)

burning, caustic, sharp, bitter

Given the opportunity to critique his enemy's new book, the spiteful critic wrote an unusually *vitriolic* review of it for the newspaper.

Synonyms: acerbic; scathing

bitter, sharp in taste or temper

Gina's *acerbic* wit and sarcasm were feared around the office.

Synonyms: biting; caustic; cutting; tart

VITRIOLIC

adj (vih tree ah lihk)

ACQUIESCE

verb (<u>aak</u> wee ehs)

someone with masterly skill; expert musician

He is a *virtuoso* conductor and has performed in all the most prestigious concert halls.

Synonyms: genius; master

to agree; to comply quietly

> The princess *acquiesced* to demands that she marry a nobleman, but she was not happy about it.

Synonyms: accede; consent; submit

VIRTUOSO

noun (vihr choo ōh soh)

ACRIMONY

noun (<u>aak</u> rih moh nee)

change or variation; ups and downs

Investors must be prepared for *vicissitudes* in the market and not panic when stock prices fall occasionally.

Synonyms: inconstancy; mutability

bitterness, animosity

> The *acrimony* the newly divorced couple showed towards each other made everyone feel uncomfortable.

Synonyms: antipathy; asperity; choler; rancor; spleen

VICISSITUDE

noun (vih sih sih tood)

ADULTERATE

verb (uh duhl tuhr ayt)

trace, remnant

Vestiges of the former tenant still remained in the apartment, although he hadn't lived there for years.

Synonyms: relic; remains; sign

to corrupt or make impure

The restaurateur made his ketchup last longer by *adulterating* it with water.

Synonyms: contaminate; dilute

VESTIGE

noun (veh stihj)

AESTHETIC

adj (ehs <u>theh</u> tihk)

quality of appearing true or real

The TV show's *verisimilitude* led viewers to believe that the characters it portrayed were real.

Synonym: reality

pertaining to beauty or art

> The museum curator, with her fine *aesthetic* sense, created an exhibit that was a joy to behold.

Synonyms: artistic; tasteful

VERISIMILITUDE

noun (vehr uh sih mihl ih tood)

AGGRANDIZE

verb (uh graan diez) (aa gruhn diez)

green with vegetation

He wandered deep into the *verdant* woods in search of mushrooms and other edible flora.

Synonyms: grassy; leafy; wooded

to make larger or greater in power

> All the millionaire really wanted was to *aggrandize* his personal wealth as much as possible.

Synonyms: advance; elevate; exalt; glorify; magnify

VERDANT

adj (vuhr dnt)

ALACRITY

noun (uh laak crih tee)

to adore; to honor; to respect

In traditional Confucian society, the young *venerate* the older members of their village, and defer to the elders' wisdom.

Synonym: regard

cheerful willingness, eagerness; speed

The eager dog fetched with *alacrity* the stick that had been tossed for him.

Synonyms: briskness; celerity; dispatch

VENERATE

verb (vehn uhr ayt)

ALLEGORY

noun (aa lih gohr ee)

boasted about, bragged about

The *vaunted* new computer program turned out to have so many bugs that it had to be recalled.

Synonyms: acclaimed; celebrated

symbolic representation

The novelist used the stormy ocean as an *allegory* for her life's struggles.

Synonyms: metaphor; symbolism

VAUNTED

adj (vawnt ehd)

AMALGAMATE

verb (uh maal guh mayt)

tasteless, dull

Todd found his blind date *vapid* and boring, and couldn't wait to get away from her.

Synonyms: inane; insipid; vacuous

to mix, combine

Giant Industries *amalgamated* with Mega Products to form Giant-Mega Products Incorporated.

Synonyms: assimilate; incorporate; integrate; league; merge

VAPID

adj (vaa pihd)

AMELIORATE

verb (uh meel yuhr ayt)

empty, void; lacking intelligence, purposeless

The politician's *vacuous* speech angered the voters, who were tired of hearing empty platitudes.

Synonyms: idle; inane; stupid; vacant

to make better; to improve

> Conditions in the hospital were *ameliorated* by the hiring of dozens of expertly trained nurses.

Synonyms: amend; better; reform

VACUOUS

adj (vaa kyoo uhs)

to waver; to show indecision

The customer held up the line as he *vacillated* between ordering chocolate or coffee ice cream.

Synonyms: falter; hesitate; oscillate; sway; waffle

AMORTIZE

verb (aam uhr tiiz) (uh mohr tiez)

to diminish by installment payments

She was able to *amortize* her debts by paying a small amount each month.

Synonym: extinguish

VACILLATE

verb (vaa sihl ayt)

ANACHRONISM

noun (uh <u>naak</u> ruh nih suhm)

KAPLAN

efficient, functional, useful

The suitcase was undeniably *utilitarian*, with its convenient compartments of different sizes.

Synonyms: practical; pragmatic

something chronologically inappropriate

> The aged hippie used *anachronisms* like “groovy” and “far out” that had not been popular for years.

Synonyms: anomalous; inappropriate; inconsistent

UTILITARIAN

adj (yoo tih lih teh ree uhn)

ANATHEMA

noun (uh naath uh muh)

to seize by force

The vice-principal was wildly ambitious, and threatened to *usurp* the principal's power.

Synonyms: appropriate; arrogate; assume

ban, curse; something shunned or disliked

Sweaty, soiled clothing was *anathema* to the elegant Madeleine.

Synonyms: abomination; aversion; execration; horror

USURP

verb (yoo suhrp)

courteous, refined, suave

The *urbane* teenager sneered at the mannerisms of his country-bumpkin cousin.

Synonyms: cosmopolitan; debonair; elegant; polite; soigné

ANCILLARY

adj (aan suhl eh ree)

accessory; subordinate; helping

> Reforms were instituted at the main factory, but not at its *ancillary* plants, so defects continued to occur.

Synonyms: addtional; adjunct; auxiliary; supplemental

URBANE

adj (uhr bayn)

ANTEDILUVIAN

adj (aan tih duh loo vee uhn)

to scold sharply

The teacher *upbraided* the student for scrawling graffiti all over the walls of the school.

Synonyms: berate; chide; rebuke; reproach; tax

prehistoric, ancient beyond measure

The *antediluvian* fossils were displayed in the museum.

Synonyms: antique; archaic; old

UPBRAID

verb (uhp brayd)

ANTERIOR

adj (aan <u>teer</u> ee uhr)

smug and falsely earnest

The *unctuous* salesman showered the rich customers with exaggerated compliments.

Synonyms: fulsome; phony; smarmy

preceding, previous, before, prior (to)

Following custom, dinner was *anterior* to the dessert.

Synonyms: foregoing; previous

KAPLAN

UNCTUOUS

adj (ungk choo uhs)

ANTIPATHY

noun (aan <u>tih</u> puh thee)

offense, resentment

The businessman took *umbrage* at the security guard's accusation that he had shoplifted a packet of gum.

Synonyms: asperity; dudgeon; ire; pique; rancor

dislike, hostility; extreme opposition or aversion

The *antipathy* between the French and the English regularly erupted into open warfare.

Synonyms: antagonism; enmity; malice

UMBRAGE

noun (uhm brihj)

APOCRYPHAL

adj (uh <u>pahk</u> ruh fuhl)

being everywhere simultaneously

Fast food franchises are *ubiquitous* in the United States, and are common in foreign countries as well.

Synonyms: inescapable; omnipresent

not genuine, fictional

Sharon suspected that the stories she was hearing about alligators in the sewer were *apocryphal.*

Synonyms: erroneous; false; fictitious; fraudulent

KAPLAN

UBIQUITOUS

adj (yoo bihk wih tuhs)

APOTHEOSIS

noun (uh pahth ee oh sihs) (aap uh thee uh sihs)

beginner, novice

An obvious *tyro* at salsa, Millicent received no invitations to dance.

Synonyms: apprentice; fledgling; greenhorn; neophyte; tenderfoot

glorification, glorified ideal

> In her heyday, many people considered Jackie Kennedy to be the *apotheosis* of stylishness.

Synonyms: epitome; ultimate

TYRO

noun (tie roh)

APPROBATION

noun (aa pruh <u>bay</u> shuhn)

state of confusion; agitation

The *tumult* of the demonstrators drowned out the police chief's speech.

Synonyms: chaos; commotion; din; disturbance; turmoil

praise, official approval

Billy was sure he had gained the *approbation* of his teacher when he received a glowing report card.

Synonyms: acclaim; accolade; applause; encomium; homage

TUMULT

noun (tuh muhlt)

ARDENT

adj (ahr dihnt)

to cut off; to shorten by cutting

The mayor *truncated* his standard lengthy speech when he realized that the audience was not in the mood to listen to it.

Synonyms: crop; curtail; lop

passionate, enthusiastic, fervent

> After a 25-game losing streak, even the Mets' most *ardent* fans realized the team wouldn't finish first.

Synonyms: fervid; intense; vehement

TRUNCATE

verb (truhnk ayt)

shallow, superficial

Lindsay's graduation speech was the same *trite* nonsense we have heard hundreds of times in the past.

Synonyms: banal; hackneyed; shopworn; stale; threadbare

noun (<u>ahr</u> duhr)

ARDOR

great emotion or passion

> Bishop's *ardor* for landscape was evident when he passionately described the beauty of the Hudson Valley.

Synonyms: enthusiasm; zeal

TRITE

adj (triet)

ARDUOUS

adj (ahr jyoo uhs) (aar dyoo uhs)

of slight worth, trivial, insignificant

That little glitch in the computer program is a *trifling* error; in general, it works very well.

Synonyms: frivolous; idle; paltry; petty; picayune

extremely difficult, laborious

> Amy thought she would pass out after completing the *arduous* climb up the mountain.

Synonyms: burdensome; hard; onerous; toilsome

TRIFLING

adj (trīe fling)

ASCETIC

adj (uh <u>seh</u> tihk)

fear and anxiety

Alana approached the door of the principal's office with *trepidation.*

Synonyms: alarm; apprehension; dread; fright

self-denying, abstinent, austere

> The monk lived an *ascetic* life deep in the wilderness, denying himself all forms of luxury.

Synonyms: abstemious; continent; temperate

TREPIDATION

noun (treh pih day shuhn)

ASPERSION

noun (uh spuhr shuhn)

acute, sharp, incisive, forceful, effective

Dan's *trenchant* observations in class made him the professor's favorite student.

Synonyms: biting; caustic; cutting; keen

false rumor, damaging report, slander

It is unfair to cast *aspersions* on someone behind his or her back.

Synonyms: allegation; insinuation; reproach

TRENCHANT

adj (trehn chuhnt)

ASSIDUOUS

adj (uh sih dee uhs)

obedient, yielding

Though it was exhausted, the *tractable* workhorse obediently dragged the carriage through the mud.

Synonyms: acquiescent; compliant; docile; governable; malleable

diligent, persistent, hard-working

> The *assiduous* chauffeur scrubbed the limousine endlessly, hoping to make a good impression on his employer.

Synonyms: industrious; steadfast; thorough

TRACTABLE

adj (traak tuh buhl)

ASSUAGE

verb (uh <u>swayj</u>) (uh <u>swayzh</u>) (uh <u>swahzh</u>)

lethargic; unable to move; dormant

After surgery, the patient was *torpid* until the anesthesia wore off.

Synonyms: apathetic; benumbed; hibernating; inactive; inert

to make less severe; to ease; to relieve

Like many people, Philip used warm milk to *assuage* his sense of sleeplessness.

Synonyms: alleviate; appease; ease; mitigate; mollify

TORPID

adj (tohr pihd)

ASTRINGENT

adj (uh strihn juhnt)

book, usually large and academic

The teacher was forced to refer to various *tomes* to find the answer to the advanced student's question.

Synonyms: codex; volume

harsh, severe, stern

> The principal's punishments seemed overly *astringent*, but the students did not dare to complain.

Synonyms: bitter; caustic; sharp

TOME

noun (tohm)

timid, shy, full of apprehension

A *timorous* woman, Lois was quiet even around her closest friends.

Synonyms: anxious; fearful; frightened

ATROCIOUS

adj (uh troh shuhs)

monstrous, shockingly bad, wicked

> The young boy committed the *atrocious* act of vandalizing the new community center.

Synonyms: appalling; deplorable; direful; horrible

TIMOROUS

adj (tih muhr uhs)

defensible, reasonable

His decision to quit his job and travel around the world was *tenable* only because he inherited millions of dollars.

Synonyms: maintainable; rational

ATROPHY

noun (aa troh fee)

to waste away; to wither from disuse

When Mimi stopped exercising, her muscles began to *atrophy*.

Synonyms: degenerate; deteriorate

TENABLE

adj (tehn uh buhl)

ATTENUATE

verb (uh <u>tehn</u> yoo ayt)

digressing, diverting

Your argument is interesting, but it's *tangential* to the matter at hand, so I suggest we get back to the point.

Synonyms: digressive; extraneous; inconsequential; irrelevant; peripheral

to weaken; to make thin or slender

> The Bill of Rights *attenuated* the traditional power of government to change laws at will.

Synonyms: diminish; rarefy; reduce

KAPLAN

TANGENTIAL

adj (taan jehn shuhl)

AUGURY

noun (aw gyuh ree) (aw guh ree)

silently understood or implied

Although not a word had been said, everyone in the room knew that a *tacit* agreement had been made about which course of action to take.

Synonyms: implicit; unspoken

prophecy, prediction of events

Troy hoped the rainbow was an *augury* of good things to come.

Synonyms: auspice; harbinger; omen; portent; presage

TACIT

adj (taa siht)

AUGUST

adj (aw <u>guhst</u>)

self-serving flatterer, yes-man

Dreading criticism, the actor surrounded himself with admirers and *sycophants.*

Synonyms: bootlicker; fawner; lickspittle; toady

dignified, awe inspiring, venerable

> The *august* view of the summit of the Grand Teton filled the climbers with awe.

Synonyms: admirable; awesome; grand; majestic

SYCOPHANT

noun (sie kuh fuhnt)

AUSPICIOUS

adj (aw <u>spih</u> shuhs)

characterized by secrecy

The queen knew nothing of the *surreptitious* plots being hatched against her at court.

Synonyms: clandestine; covert; furtive

having favorable prospects, promising

> Tamika thought that having lunch with the boss was an *auspicious* start to her new job.

Synonyms: encouraging; hopeful; positive; propitious

SURREPTITIOUS

adj (suh rehp tih shuhs)

AVARICE

noun (aa vuhr ihs)

excessive amount

Because of the *surfeit* of pigs, pork prices have never been lower.

Synonyms: glut; plethora; repletion; superfluity; surplus

greed

Rebecca's *avarice* motivated her to stuff the $100 bill in her pocket instead of returning it to the man who had dropped it.

Synonyms: cupidity; rapacity

SURFEIT

noun (suhr fiht)

AXIOM

noun (<u>aak</u> see uhm)

arrogant, haughty, overbearing, condescending

She was a shallow and scornful society woman with a *supercilious* manner.

Synonyms: disdainful; patronizing; proud

premise, postulate, self-evident truth

Halle lived her life based on the *axioms* her grandmother had passed on to her.

Synonyms: adage; aphorism; apothegm; maxim; rule

SUPERCILIOUS

adj (soo puhr sihl ee uhs)

BALEFUL

adj (<u>bayl</u> fuhl)

too old, obsolete, outdated

The manual typewriter has become *superannuated*, although a few loyal diehards still swear by it.

Synonyms: disused; outworn

harmful, with evil intentions

The sullen teenager gave his nagging mother a *baleful* look.

Synonyms: dark; sinister

SUPERANNUATED

adj (soo puhr aan yoo ay tihd)

trick or tactic used to avoid something

Spies who are not skilled in the art of *subterfuge* are generally exposed before too long.

Synonyms: ruse; stratagem

BANAL

adj (buh naal) (bay nuhl) (buh nahl)

trite, overly common

He used *banal* phrases like “Have a nice day” or “Another day, another dollar.”

Synonyms: hackneyed; inane; shopworn

SUBTERFUGE

noun (suhb tuhr fyooj)

BASTION

noun (<u>baas</u> chyuhn) (<u>baas</u> tee uhn)

to enslave; to conquer, subdue

The Romans *subjugated* all the peoples they conquered.

Synonyms: defeat; enthrall; vanquish; yoke

fortification, stronghold

The club was well known as a *bastion* of conservative values in the liberal city.

Synonyms: bulwark; defense; haven

SUBJUGATE

verb (suhb juh gayt)

BELABOR

verb (bih lay buhr)

to impair or reduce to uselessness

The company's leadership was *stultified* by its practice of promoting the owner's incapable children to powerful positions.

Synonyms: damage; mar

to insist repeatedly or harp on

I understand completely; you do not need to *belabor* the point.

Synonyms: dwell upon; lambaste

STULTIFY

verb (stuhl tuh fie)

BELEAGUER

verb (bih lee guhr)

having or showing little emotion

The prisoner appeared *stolid* and unaffected by the judge's harsh sentence.

Synonyms: impassive; stoic

to harass, plague

> Mickey *beleaguered* his parents until they finally gave in to his request for a new computer.

Synonyms: beset; besiege

STOLID

adj (stah lihd)

BELIE

verb (bih lie)

indifferent to or unaffected by emotions

While most of the mourners wept, the dead woman's husband kept up a *stoic*, unemotional façade.

Synonyms: impassive; stolid

to misrepresent; to expose as false

> The first lady's carefree appearance *belied* rumors that she was on the verge of divorcing her husband.

Synonyms: distort; refute

STOIC

adj (stoh ihk)

warlike, aggressive

> Immediately after defeating one of his enemies, the *bellicose* chieftain declared war on another.

Synonyms: belligerent; combative; hostile; pugnacious

STAID

adj (stayd)

BELLICOSE

adj (<u>beh</u> lih cohs)

self-restrained to the point of dullness

The lively young girl felt bored in the company of her *staid*, conservative date.

Synonyms: grave; sedate; serious; sober; solemn

BELLIGERENT

adj (buh lih juhr uhnt)

lacking authenticity; counterfeit, false

Quoting from a *spurious* document, the employee declared that all profits should be signed over to him.

Synonyms: ersatz; fake; fraudulent; mock; phony

hostile, tending to fight

> The angry customer was extremely *belligerent* despite the manager's offer to return his money.

Synonyms: agressive; bellicose; combative; pugnacious

SPURIOUS

adj (spyoor ee uhs)

BENIGHTED

adj (bih <u>nie</u> tihd)

sleepy or tending to cause sleep

The movie proved to be so *soporific* that loud snores were heard throughout the theater.

Synonyms: drowsy; narcotic; somniferous; somnolent

unenlightened

> Ben scoffed at the crowd, as he believed it consisted entirely of *benighted* individuals.

Synonyms: ignorant; illiterate; unschooled

SOPORIFIC

adj (sahp uhr ihf ihk)

BEQUEATH

verb (bih kweeth)

deceptive reasoning or argumentation

The politician used *sophistry* to cloud the issue whenever he was asked a tough question in a debate.

Synonym: cogitation

to give or leave through a will; to hand down

Grandpa *bequeathed* the house to his daughter and the car to his son.

Synonyms: bestow; pass on; transmit

SOPHISTRY

noun (sahf ih stree)

BESEECH

verb (bih seech)

producing a full, rich sound

The *sonorous* blaring of the foghorn woke up Lily at 4:30 in the morning.

Synonyms: orotund; resonant; vibrant

to beg, plead, implore

She *beseeched* him to give her a second chance, but he refused.

Synonyms: entreat; petition; supplicate

SONOROUS

adj (sah nuhr uhs)

BILK

verb (bihlk)

drowsy, sleepy; inducing sleep

Carter became *somnolent* after he ate a huge meal.

Synonyms: sluggish; slumberous; somniferous; soporific

to cheat, defraud

> Though the lawyer seemed honest, the woman feared he would try to *bilk* her out of her money.

Synonyms: dupe; fleece; swindle

SOMNOLENT

adj (sahm nuh luhnt)

BLANDISH

verb (<u>blaan</u> dihsh)

belief that oneself is the only reality

Arthur's *solipsism* annoyed others, since he treated them as if they didn't exist.

Synonym: self-interest

to coax with flattery

We *blandished* the teacher with compliments until he finally agreed to postpone the exam.

Synonyms: cajole; charm; wheedle

SOLIPSISM

noun (sahl ihp sihz uhm) (sohl ihp sihz uhm)

BLIGHT

verb (bliet)

grammatical mistake

The applicant's letter was filled with embarrassing *solecisms*, such as "I works here at 20 years."

Synonym: language blunder

to afflict; to destroy

> The farmers feared that the previous night's frost had *blighted* the potato crops entirely.

Synonyms: damage; plague

SOLECISM

noun (sahl ih sihz uhm) (sohl ih sihz uhm)

BONHOMIE

noun (bahn uh mee)

winding; intricate, complex

Thick, *sinuous* vines wound around the trunk of the tree.

Synonyms: curvilinear; lithe; serpentine; supple

good-natured geniality; atmosphere of good cheer

The general *bonhomie* that characterized the party made it a joy to attend.

Synonym: friendliness

SINUOUS

adj (sihn yoo uhs)

to smirk; to smile foolishly

The spoiled girl *simpered* as her mother praised her extravagantly at the party.

Synonyms: grin; smirk

BOON

noun

blessing, something to be thankful for

> Dirk realized that his new coworker's computer skills would be a real *boon* to the company.

Synonyms: benefit; favor; treasure; windfall

SIMPER

verb (sihm puhr)

angelic, pure, sublime

Selena's sweet, *seraphic* appearance belied her nasty, bitter personality.

Synonyms: cherubic; heavenly

BOURGEOIS

adj (boor zhwaa) (boo zhwaa) (buh zhwaa)

middle class

> The *bourgeois* family was horrified when the lower-class family moved in next door.

Synonyms: capitalist; conventional

SERAPHIC

adj (seh rah fihk)

BREACH

noun (breech)

aware, conscious, able to perceive

Despite his complete lack of sleep, Jorge was still *sentient* when I spoke to him this morning.

Synonyms: feeling; intelligent; thinking

act of breaking, violation

The record company sued the singer for *breach* of contract when he recorded for another company without permission.

Synonyms: contravention; dereliction; gap; lapse; rift

SENTIENT

adj (sehn shuhnt)

having a moralizing tone

The principal took on a *sententious* tone when he lectured the students on their inappropriate behavior during the school assembly.

Synonyms: aphoristic; moralistic; pithy; pompous; terse

BRIGAND

noun (brihg uhnd)

bandit, outlaw

Brigands held up the bank and made off with the contents of the safe.

Synonym: plunderer

SENTENTIOUS

adj (sehn tehn shuhs)

BRUSQUE

adj (bruhsk)

old

Fearful of becoming *senescent*, Jobim worked out several times a week and ate only healthy foods.

Synonyms: aged; mature

rough and abrupt in manner

The bank teller's *brusque* treatment of his customers soon evoked several complaints.

Synonyms: blunt; curt; gruff; rude; tactless

SENESCENT

adj (sih nehs uhnt)

BURGEON

verb (buhr juhn)

narrow-minded; relating to a group or sect

Since the fall of Communism in the former Yugoslavia, its various ethnic groups have plunged into *sectarian* violence.

Synonym: schismatic

to sprout or flourish

> Because the population of the city is *burgeoning*, we are going to need a major subway expansion.

Synonyms: blossom; expand; grow; proliferate; thrive

SECTARIAN

adj (sehk tayr ee uhn)

BUTTRESS

verb (<u>buh</u> trihs)

vulgar, low, indecent

The decadent aristocrat took part in *scurrilous* activities every night, unbeknownst to his family.

Synonyms: abusive; coarse; foul-mouthed

to reinforce or support

> The construction workers attempted to *buttress* the crumbling ceiling with pillars.

Synonyms: bolster; brace; prop; strengthen

SCURRILOUS

adj (skuh ruh luhs)

CADENCE

noun (kayd ns)

to sparkle, flash

The society hostess was famous for throwing parties that *scintillated* and impressed every guest.

Synonyms: gleam; glisten; glitter; shimmer; twinkle

rhythmic flow of poetry; marching beat

Pierre spoke with a lovely *cadence*, charming all those who heard him.

Synonyms: inflection; rhythm

SCINTILLATE

verb (sihn tuhl ayt)

trace amount

This poison is so powerful that no more than a *scintilla* of it is needed to kill a horse.

Synonyms: atom; iota; mote; spark; speck

CAJOLE

verb (kuh <u>johl</u>)

to flatter, coax, persuade

The spoiled girl could *cajole* her father into buying her anything.

Synonyms: blandish; wheedle

SCINTILLA

noun (sihn tihl uh)

CALLOW

adj (<u>kaa</u> loh)

cynical, scornfully mocking

Denise was offended by the *sardonic* way in which her date made fun of her ideas and opinions.

Synonyms: acerbic; caustic; sarcastic; satirical; snide

immature, lacking sophistication

The young and *callow* fans hung on every word the talk show host said.

Synonyms: artless; ingenuous; naïve

SARDONIC

adj (sahr dah nihk)

CAPACIOUS

adj (kuh <u>pay</u> shuhs)

cheerfully optimistic; ruddy

A *sanguine* person thinks the glass is half full, while a depressed person thinks it's half empty.

Synonyms: confident; hopeful; positive; rosy; rubicund

large, roomy; extensive

We wondered how many hundreds of stores occupied the *capacious* mall.

Synonyms: ample; commodious

SANGUINE

adj (saan gwuhn)

CAPITULATE

verb (kuh pih choo layt)

healthful

Rundown and sickly, Rita hoped that the fresh mountain air would have a *salubrious* effect on her health.

Synonyms: bracing; curative; medicinal; therapeutic; tonic

to submit completely, surrender

After the army was reduced to only five soldiers, there was little choice but to *capitulate.*

Synonyms: acquiesce; succumb; yield

SALUBRIOUS

adj (suh loo bree uhs)

CAPRICIOUS

adj (kuh <u>pree</u> shuhs) (kuh <u>prih</u> shuhs)

shrewd, keen

Aimee has a reputation for being a *sagacious* businessperson; she is always one step ahead of her competitors.

Synonyms: astute; judicious; perspicacious; sage; wise

impulsive, whimsical, without much thought

> Queen Elizabeth I was quite *capricious*; her courtiers could never be sure who would catch her fancy.

Synonyms: erratic; fickle; flighty; inconstant; wayward

SAGACIOUS

adj (suh gay shuhs)

CASTIGATE

verb (<u>kaa</u> stih gayt)

extremely sacred; beyond criticism

Many people considered Mother Teresa to be *sacrosanct* and would not tolerate any criticism of her.

Synonyms: holy; inviolable; off-limits

to punish; to chastise, to criticize severely

> Authorities in Singapore harshly *castigate* perpetrators of what would be considered minor crimes in the United States.

Synonyms: discipline; lambaste

SACROSANCT

adj (saa kroh saankt)

CATHARSIS

noun (kuh <u>thahr</u> sihs)

to contemplate, reflect upon

The scholars spent days at the retreat *ruminating* upon the complexities of the geopolitical situation.

Synonyms: deliberate; meditate; mull; muse; ponder

purification, cleansing

> Plays can be more satisfying if they end in some sort of emotional *catharsis* for the characters involved.

Synonyms: purgation; release

RUMINATE

verb (roo muh nayt)

CATHOLIC

adj (kaa thuh lihk) (kaa thlihk)

---

to make many holes in; to permeate

The gunfire *riddled* the helicopter with thousands of holes.

Synonyms: honeycomb; perforate; pierce; prick; punch

universal; broad and comprehensive

Hot tea with honey is a *catholic* remedy for a sore throat.

Synonyms: extensive; general

RIDDLE

verb (rih duhl)

CAVALIER

adj (kaav uh leer)

humorous in a vulgar way

The court jester's *ribald* brand of humor delighted the rather uncouth king.

Synonyms: coarse; gross; indelicate; obscene

carefree, happy; with lordly disdain

> The nobleman's *cavalier* attitude towards the suffering of the peasants made them hate him.

Synonym: apathetic

RIBALD

adj (rīh buhld)

CENTRIPETAL

adj (sehn <u>trihp</u> ih tl)

boisterous festivity

An atmosphere of *revelry* filled the school after its basketball team's surprising victory.

Synonyms: cavorting; gaiety; jollity; merrymaking

directed or moving towards the center

It is *centripetal* force that keeps trains from derailing as they round curves.

Synonym: centralizing

KAPLAN

REVELRY

noun (reh vuhl ree)

CHAGRIN

noun (shuh <u>grihn</u>)

to cut down; to reduce

The most recent round of layoffs *retrenched* our staff to only three people.

Synonyms: excise; remove; shorten

shame, embarrassment, humiliation

> No doubt, the president felt a good deal of *chagrin* after forgetting the name of the prime minister at the state banquet.

Synonyms: discomfiture; mortification

RETRENCH

verb (rih trehnch)

CHARLATAN

noun (<u>shahr</u> luh tihn)

shy, modest, reserved

A shy and *retiring* man, Chuck was horrified at the idea of having to speak in public.

Synonym: timid

quack, fake

> "That *charlatan* of a doctor prescribed the wrong medicine for me!" complained the patient.

Synonyms: fraud; humbug; imposter

RETIRING

adj (rih tier ihng)

CHICANERY

noun (shih kayn ree) (shi kay nuh ree) (“ch” can replace “sh”)

group of attendants with an important person

The nobleman had to make room in his mansion for the princess, and for her entire *retinue*.

Synonyms: entourage; following

trickery, fraud, deception

Dishonest used car salesmen often use *chicanery* to sell their beat-up old cars.

Synonyms: deceit; dishonesty; duplicity

RETINUE

noun (reht noo)

CHOLERIC

adj (kah luhr ihk)

not speaking freely; reserved

Physically small and *reticent*, Joan Didion often went unnoticed by those upon whom she was reporting.

Synonyms: restrained; secretive; silent; taciturn

easily angered, short-tempered

The *choleric* principal raged at the students who had come late to school.

Synonyms: irate; irritable; surly; wrathful

RETICENT

adj (reh tih suhnt)

CIRCUMLOCUTION

noun (suhr kuhm loh <u>kyoo</u> shuhn)

impatient, uneasy, restless

The customers became *restive* after having to wait in line for hours.

Synonyms: agitated; anxious; fretful

roundabout, lengthy way of saying something

He avoided discussing the real issues with endless *circumlocution*.

Synonyms: evasion; wordiness

RESTIVE

adj (reh stihv)

CIRCUMSCRIBE

verb (suhr kuhm skrieb)

to reject as having no authority

The old woman's claim that she was Russian royalty was *repudiated* when DNA tests showed she was not related to them.

Synonyms: abjure; disclaim; disown; forswear; renounce

to encircle; to set limits on, confine

Diego Buenaventura's country estate is *circumscribed* by rolling hills.

Synonyms: limit; surround

REPUDIATE

verb (rih pyoo dee ayt)

CIRCUMSPECT

adj (suhr kuhm spehkt)

morally unprincipled person

If you ignore your society's accepted moral code, you will be considered a *reprobate.*

Synonyms: knave; rake; rogue; scoundrel; sinner

cautious, wary

His failures made Jack far more *circumspect* in his exploits than he used to be.

Synonyms: careful; chary; prudent

REPROBATE

noun (reh pruh bayt)

CLANDESTINE

adj (klaan dehs tien)

capable of being corrected

In the belief that the juvenile delinquent was *remediable* the judge put him on probation.

Synonym: fixable

secretive, concealed for a darker purpose

> The double agent paid many *clandestine* visits to the president's office in the dead of night.

Synonyms: covert; underground

REMEDIABLE

adj (rih mee dee uh buhl)

response

Patrick tried desperately to think of a clever *rejoinder* to Marcy's joke, but he couldn't.

Synonyms: retort; riposte

CLEMENCY

noun (kleh muhn see)

merciful leniency

Kyle begged for *clemency*, explaining that he robbed the bank to pay for his medical bills.

Synonyms: indulgence; pardon

REJOINDER

noun (rih joyn duhr)

COALESCE

verb (koh uh lehs)

relief from wrong or injury

Seeking *redress* for the injuries she had received in the accident, Doreen sued the driver of the truck that had hit her.

Synonyms: amends; indemnity; quittance; reparation; restitution

to grow together or cause to unite as one

> The different factions of the organization *coalesced* to form one united front against their opponents.

Synonyms: combine; merge

REDRESS

noun (rih drehs)

COLLATERAL

adj (kuh laat uhr uhl)

moral uprightness

Young women used to be shipped off to finishing schools to teach them proper manners and *rectitude*.

Synonyms: honesty; honor; integrity; probity; righteousness

accompanying

> "Let's try to stick to the main issue here and not get into all the *collateral* questions," urged the committee leader.

Synonym: ancillary

RECTITUDE

noun (rehk tih tood)

COLLOQUY

noun (kahl uh kwee)

relating to obscure learning; known to only a few

The ideas expressed in the ancient philosophical treatise were so *recondite* that only a few scholars could appreciate them.

Synonym: esoteric

dialogue or conversation; conference

The congressmen held a *colloquy* to determine how to proceed with the environmental legislation.

Synonym: discussion

RECONDITE

adj (rehk uhn diet) (rih kahn diet)

COLLUSION

noun (kuh loo zhuhn)

to retract a statement, opinion, etc.

The statement was so damaging that the politician had no hopes of recovering his credibility, even though he tried to *recant* the words.

Synonyms: disavow; disclaim; disown; renounce; repudiate

collaboration, complicity, conspiracy

> The teacher realized that the students were in *collusion* when everyone received the same grade on the test.

Synonyms: connivance; intrigue; machination

RECANT

verb (ree kant)

COMELINESS

noun (kuhm lee nihs)

resisting authority or control

The *recalcitrant* mule refused to go down the treacherous path, however hard its master pulled at its reins.

Synonyms: defiant; headstrong; stubborn; unruly; willful

physical grace and beauty

Ann's *comeliness* made her perfect for the role of Sleeping Beauty.

Synonyms: attractiveness; seemliness

RECALCITRANT

adj (ree kaal sih truhnt)

COMMENSURATE

adj (kuh mehn suhr ayt)

witty, skillful storyteller

The *raconteur* kept all the passengers entertained with his stories during the six-hour flight.

Synonyms: anecdotalist; monologist

proportional

Steve was given a salary *commensurate* with his experience.

Synonyms: comparable; corresponding

RACONTEUR

noun (raa cahn tuhr)

COMMODIOUS

adj (kuh moh dee uhs)

occurring daily; commonplace

The sight of people singing on the street is so *quotidian* in New York that passersby rarely react to it.

Synonyms: everyday; normal; usual

roomy, spacious

Raqiyah was able to stretch out fully in the *commodious* bathtub.

Synonyms: ample; capacious; extensive

QUOTIDIAN

adj (kwo tih dee uhn)

COMPLICITY

noun (kuhm plih sih tee)

overly idealistic, impractical

The practical Danuta was skeptical of her roommate's *quixotic* plans to build an amphitheater in their yard.

Synonyms: capricious; impulsive; romantic; unrealistic

knowing partnership in wrongdoing

> The two boys exchanged a look of sly *complicity* when their father shouted "Who broke the window?"

Synonyms: cahoots; collaboration; involvement

QUIXOTIC

adj (kwihk sah tihk)

COMPUNCTION

noun (kuhm puhnk shuhn)

inactivity, stillness

Bears fall into a state of *quiescence* when they hibernate during the winter months.

Synonyms: calm; dormancy; idleness; repose

feeling of uneasiness caused by guilt or regret

> Her *compunction* was intense when she realized that she forgot to send her best friend a birthday card.

Synonyms: dubiety; qualm; scruple

QUIESCENCE

noun (kwie e̱h sihns)

CONCILIATORY

adj (kuhn sihl ee uh tohr ee)

inclined to complain, irritable

Curtis's complaint received prompt attention after the company labeled him a *querulous* customer.

Synonyms: peevish; puling; whiny; sniveling

overcoming distrust or hostility

Fred made the *conciliatory* gesture of buying Abby flowers after their big fight.

Synonym: pleasing

QUERULOUS

adj (kwehr yoo luhs)

CONGENITAL

adj (kuhn jehn ih tl)

difficult situation; marsh

Oliver realized that he needed help to get himself out of this *quagmire*.

Synonyms: bog; fen; mire; morass; swamp

existing since birth

The infant's *congenital* health problem was corrected through surgery.

Synonym: innate

QUAGMIRE

noun (kwaag mier)

CONGRUITY

noun (kuhn <u>groo</u> ih tee)

---

beauty

The mortals gazed in admiration at Venus, stunned by her incredible *pulchritude.*

Synonyms: comeliness; gorgeousness; handsomeness; loveliness; prettiness

correspondence, harmony, agreement

There was an obvious *congruity* between Marco's pleasant personality and his kind actions toward others.

Synonym: accord

PULCHRITUDE

noun (puhl kruh tood)

CONJECTURE

noun (kuhn jehk shuhr)

---

quarrelsome, eager and ready to fight

The serene eighty-year-old used to be a *pugnacious* troublemaker in her youth, but she's softer now.

Synonyms: bellicose; belligerent; contentious

speculation, prediction

The actor refused to comment, forcing gossip columnists to make *conjectures* on his love life.

Synonyms: hypothesis; postulation; supposition

PUGNACIOUS

adj (pug nay shus)

CONJURE

verb (<u>kahn</u> juhr) (kuhn <u>joor</u>)

boxing

Pugilism has been defended as a positive outlet for aggressive impulses.

Synonyms: fighting; sparring

to evoke; to cast a spell

> The cotton candy *conjured* up the image of the fairgrounds he used to visit as a child in Arthur's mind.

Synonym: summon

PUGILISM

noun (pyoo juhl ih suhm)

CONSONANT

adj (kahn suh nuhnt)

childish, immature, silly

His *puerile* antics are really annoying; sometimes he acts like a five-year-old!

Synonyms: infantile; jejune; juvenile

consistent with, in agreement with

> The pitiful raise Ingrid received was *consonant* with the low opinion her manager had of her performance.

Synonyms: accordant; compatible; congruous

PUERILE

adj (pyoo ruhl)

CONSTRUE

verb (kuhn <u>stroo</u>)

readily assuming different forms or characters

The *protean* actor could play a wide variety of different characters convincingly.

Synonym: versatile

to interpret or explain

> "I wasn't sure how to *construe* that last remark he made," said Delia, "but I suspect it was an insult."

Synonyms: analyze; translate

PROTEAN

adj (proh tee uhn)

CONSUMMATE

adj (<u>kahn</u> suh muht) (<u>kahn</u> soo miht)

to convert to a particular belief or religion

The religious group went from door to door in the neighborhood, *proselytizing* enthusiastically.

Synonyms: convince; missionize; move; preach; sway

accomplished, complete, perfect

The skater delivered a *consummate* performance, perfect in every aspect.

Synonyms: exhaustive; flawless; ideal; thorough

PROSELYTIZE

verb (prah suhl uh tiez)

CONTINENCE

noun (<u>kahn</u> tih nihns)

favorable, advantageous

"I realize that I should have brought this up at a more *propitious* moment, but I don't love you," said the bride to the groom in the middle of their marriage vows.

Synonyms: auspicious; benign; conducive

self-control, self-restraint

> Lucy exhibited impressive *continence* in steering clear of fattening foods; as a result, she lost 50 pounds.

Synonyms: discipline; moderation

PROPITIOUS

adj (pruh pih shuhs)

CONTRAVENE

verb (kahn truh veen)

nearness

The house's *propinquity* to the foul-smelling pig farm made it impossible to sell.

Synonym: proximity

to contradict, deny, act contrary to

> The watchman *contravened* his official instructions by leaving his post for an hour.

Synonyms: disobey; transgress; violate

PROPINQUITY

noun (pruh pihng kwih tee)

CONVIVIAL

adj (kuhn <u>vihv</u> ee uhl)

corrupt, degenerate

Some historians claim that it was the Romans' decadent, *profligate* behavior that led to the decline of the Roman Empire.

Synonyms: dissolute; extravagant; improvident; prodigal; wasteful

sociable; fond of eating, drinking, and people

> The restaurant's *convivial* atmosphere contrasted starkly with the gloom of Maureen's empty apartment.

Synonym: companionable

PROFLIGATE

adj (praa flih guht)

CONVOKE

verb (kuhn vohk)

vast, enormous, extraordinary

The musician's *prodigious* talent made her famous all over the world.

Synonyms: gigantic; huge; impressive; marvelous

to call together, summon

The president *convoked* a group of experts to advise him on how to deal with the crisis.

Synonyms: assemble; convene; gather

PRODIGIOUS

adj (pruh dih juhs)

CONVOLUTED

adj (kahn vuh loo tehd)

tendency, inclination

His *proclivity* for speeding got him into trouble with the highway patrol on many occasions.

Synonyms: partiality; penchant; predilection; predisposition; propensity

twisted, complicated, involved

> Although many people bought *A Brief History of Time*, few could follow its *convoluted* ideas and theories.

Synonyms: baroque; elaborate; intricate

PROCLIVITY

noun (proh clih vuh tee)

COPIOUS

adj (<u>koh</u> pee uhs)

honesty, high-mindedness

The conscientious witness responded with the utmost *probity* to all the questions posed to her.

Synonyms: honor; integrity; rectitude; uprightness; virtue

abundant, plentiful

The hostess had prepared *copious* amounts of food for the banquet.

Synonyms: abounding; ample

PROBITY

noun (proh buh tee)

CORPOREAL

adj (kohr pohr ee uhl)

lack of usual necessities or comforts

The prisoner endured total *privation* while locked up in solitary confinement.

Synonyms: deprivation; forfeiture; loss; poverty

tangible, material; having to do with the body

> Makiko realized that the problem was *corporeal* in nature; it was not just an intangible issue.

Synonyms: concrete; physical; somatic

PRIVATION

noun (prih vay shuhn)

CORPULENCE

noun (kohr pyuh luhns)

to lie; to evade the truth

Rather than admit that he had overslept again, the employee *prevaricated*, claiming that traffic had made him late.

Synonyms: equivocate; fabricate; fib; hedge; palter

obesity, fatness, bulkiness

> Egbert's *corpulence* increased as he spent several hours each day eating and drinking.

Synonyms: plumpness; portliness; rotundity; stoutness

PREVARICATE

verb (prih vaar uh cayt)

CORROBORATE

verb (kuh <u>rahb</u> uhr ayt)

having foresight

Jonah's decision to sell the apartment turned out to be a *prescient* one, as its value soon dropped by half.

Synonyms: augural; divinatory; mantic; oracular; premonitory

to confirm, verify

> Roberto was able to *corroborate* his friend's story by showing the receipt that proved they were at a restaurant all night.

Synonyms: confirm; prove; substantiate; warrant

PRESCIENT

adj (preh shuhnt)

COSSET

verb (<u>kahs</u> iht)

preference, liking

The old woman's *predilection* for candy was evident from the chocolate bar wrappers strewn all over her apartment.

Synonyms: bias; leaning; partiality; penchant; proclivity

to pamper; to treat with great care

Mimi *cosseted* her toy poodle, feeding it gourmet meals and buying it a silk pillow to sleep on.

Synonym: spoil

PREDILECTION

noun (preh dih lehk shuhn)

COUNTENANCE

noun (kown tuh nuhns)

to cause to happen; to throw down from a height

It's fairly certain that Lloyd's incessant smoking *precipitated* his early death from emphysema.

Synonym: effect

facial expression; look of approval or support

> Jeremy was afraid of the new Music Appreciation instructor because she had such an evil *countenance*.

Synonyms: face; expression

PRECIPITATE

verb (preh sih puh tayt)

COUNTENANCE

verb (kown tuh nuhns)

sudden and unexpected

Since the couple wed after knowing each other only a month, many expected their *precipitate* marriage to end in divorce.

Synonyms: abrupt; headlong; impetuous; rash; reckless

to favor, support

When the girls started a pillow fight, the baby-sitter warned them, “I will not *countenance* such behavior.”

Synonyms: approve; tolerate

PRECIPITATE

adj (preh sih puh tayt)

COUNTERMAND

verb (<u>kown</u> tuhr maand)

to speak in a pretentious manner

She *pontificated* about the virtues of being rich until we all left the room in disgust.

Synonyms: declaim; lecture; orate; preach; sermonize

to annul, cancel; to make a contrary order

> Residents were relieved when the councilmembers *countermanded* the rule of 30-minute parking on all city streets.

Synonym: revoke

PONTIFICATE

verb (pahn tih fih kayt)

CRAVEN

adj (kray vuhn)

controversy, argument; verbal attack

The candidate's *polemic* against his opponent was vicious and small-minded rather than well reasoned and convincing.

Synonyms: denunciation; refutation

cowardly

The *craven* lion was terrified of the mouse.

Synonyms: faint-hearted; spineless; timid

POLEMIC

noun (puh leh mihk)

CREDENCE

noun (<u>kreed</u> ns)

to join together; to use diligently; to engage

The weaver *plied* the fibers together to make a blanket.

Synonyms: handle; manipulate

acceptance of something as true or real

> Mr. Bagley couldn't give any *credence* to the charge that his darling son had cheated on his test.

Synonym: credibility

PLY

verb (plie)

CREDULOUS

adj (<u>kreh</u> juh luhs)

to soothe or pacify

The burglar tried to *placate* the snarling Doberman by saying, "Nice doggy" and offering it a treat.

Synonyms: appease; conciliate; mollify

gullible, trusting

> Although some 4-year-olds believe in the Easter Bunny, only the most *credulous* 9-year-olds do.

Synonyms: naïve; uncritical

PLACATE

verb (play cayt)

CRESCENDO

noun (kruh shehn doh)

meager amount or wage

Zack felt sure he would not be able to buy enough food for his large family with the *pittance* the government gave him.

Synonyms: insufficiency; scrap

gradual increase

> The *crescendo* of tension became unbearable as Evel Knievel prepared to jump his motorcycle over the school buses.

Synonym: climax

PITTANCE

noun (piht ns)

profound, substantial; concise, succinct, to the point

Martha's *pithy* comments during the interview must have been impressive, because she got the job.

Synonyms: brief; compact; laconic; terse

CULPABLE

adj (<u>kuhl</u> puh buhl)

guilty, responsible for wrong-doing

The CEO is *culpable* for the bankruptcy of the company; he was, after all, in charge of it.

Synonyms: answerable; blameworthy

PITHY

adj (pīh thee)

CUPIDITY

noun (kyoo <u>pih</u> dih tee)

to steal

Marianne *pilfered* the money and spent it on a new car.

Synonyms: arrogate; embezzle; filch; poach; purloin

greed

> The poverty-stricken man stared at the shining jewels with *cupidity* in his gleaming eyes.

Synonyms: avarice; covetousness; rapacity

PILFER

verb (pihl fuhr)

CURMUDGEON

noun (kuhr <u>muh</u> juhn)

sluggish; calm in temperament

The *phlegmatic* old boar snoozed in the grass as the energetic piglets frolicked around him.

Synonyms: matter-of-fact; undemonstrative

cranky person

The old man was a notorious *curmudgeon* who snapped at anyone who disturbed him for any reason.

Synonyms: coot; crab; grouch

PHLEGMATIC

adj (flehg maa tihk)

CURSORY

adj (<u>kuhr</u> suh ree)

rudeness, peevishness

The child's *petulance* annoyed the teacher, who liked her students to be cheerful and cooperative.

Synonyms: fretfulness; irritability; querulousness; testiness

hastily done, superficial

The copyeditor gave the article a *cursory* once-over, missing dozens of errors.

Synonyms: careless; shallow

PETULANCE

noun (peh chu luhns)

DAUNT

verb (dawnt)

epidemic, plague

The country was in crisis when it was plagued by both *pestilence* and floods at the same time.

Synonyms: contagion; disease; illness; scourge; sickness

to discourage; to intimidate

She tried hard not to let the enormity of the situation *daunt* her.

Synonyms: consternate; demoralize; dishearten

PESTILENCE

noun (peh stihl ehns)

DEBASE

verb (dih <u>bays</u>)

persistent, stubborn

Despite her parents' opposition, Tina was *pertinacious* in her insistence to travel alone.

Synonym: obstinate

to degrade or lower in quality or stature

The president's deceitful actions *debased* the stature of his office.

Synonyms: adulterate; defile; demean; denigrate

PERTINACIOUS

adj (puhr tn ay shuhs)

DEBILITATE

verb (dih bih lih tayt)

shrewd, astute, keen-witted

Inspector Poirot used his *perspicacious* mind to solve mysteries.

Synonyms: insightful; intelligent; sagacious

to weaken, enfeeble

The flu d*ebilitated* the postal worker; she was barely able to finish her rounds.

Synonyms: devitalize; drain; enervate; exhaust; sap

PERSPICACIOUS

adj (puhr spuh kay shuhs)

DEBUNK

verb (dih buhnk)

very harmful

Poor nutrition and lack of exercise has a *pernicious* effect on the human body.

Synonyms: deadly; destructive; evil; pestilent; wicked

to discredit; to disprove

> It was the teacher's mission in life to *debunk* the myth that females are bad at math.

Synonyms: belie; confute; contradict; controvert

PERNICIOUS

adj (puhr nih shuhs)

DECIDUOUS

adj (dih <u>sih</u> joo uhs)

penetrable

Karen discovered that her raincoat was *permeable* when she was drenched while wearing it in a rainstorm.

Synonyms: pervious; porous

losing leaves in the fall; short-lived, temporary

> *Deciduous* trees are bare in winter, which is why evergreens are used during winter holidays.

Synonym: ephemeral

PERMEABLE

adj (puhr mee uh buhl)

DECLIVITY

noun (dih <u>klih</u> vih tee)

moving from place to place

Morty claims that his *peripatetic* hot dog stand gives him the opportunity to travel all over the city.

Synonyms: itinerant; nomadic; vagabond

downward slope

Because the village was situated on the *declivity* of a hill, it never flooded.

Synonyms: decline; descent; grade; slant; tilt

PERIPATETIC

adj (peh ruh puh teh tihk)

done in a routine way; indifferent

The machinelike bank teller processed the transaction and gave the waiting customer a *perfunctory* smile.

Synonyms: careless; halfhearted; tepid

DECOROUS

adj (deh kuhr uhs) (deh kohr uhs)

proper, tasteful, socially correct

> The socialite trained her daughters in the finer points of *decorous* behavior, hoping they would make a good impression at the debutante ball.

Synonyms: appropriate; comme il faut; courteous; polite

PERFUNCTORY

adj (puhr fuhnk tor ee)

DECRY

verb (dih crie)

faithless, disloyal, untrustworthy

The actress's *perfidious* companion revealed all of her intimate secrets to the gossip columnist.

Synonyms: deceitful; devious; treacherous

to belittle; to openly condemn

> Governments all over the world *decried* the dictator's vicious massacre of the helpless citizens.

Synonyms: depreciate; deride; derogate; disparage; minimize

PERFIDIOUS

adj (puhr fih dee uhs)

DEFERENTIAL

adj (dehf uh rehn shuhl)

complete and utter loss; damnation

Faust brought *perdition* upon himself when he made a deal with the devil in exchange for power.

Synonym: abyss

respectful and polite in a submissive way

The respectful young law clerk was *deferential* to the Supreme Court justice.

Synonyms: courteous; obsequious

PERDITION

noun (puhr dihsh uhn)

DEFT

adj (dehft)

discerning, able to perceive

The *percipient* detective saw through the suspect's lies and uncovered the truth.

Synonyms: insightful; perceptive

skillful, dexterous

It was a pleasure to watch the *deft* carpenter as he repaired the furniture.

Synonyms: adept; adroit; expert; nimble; proficient

PERCIPIENT

adj (puhr sihp ee uhnt)

DELETERIOUS

adj (dehl ih teer ee uhs)

having bad connotations; disparaging

The teacher scolded Mark for his unduly *pejorative* comments about his classmate's presentation.

Synonyms: belittling; dismissive; insulting

harmful, destructive, detrimental

> If we put these defective clocks on the market, it could be quite *deleterious* to our reputation.

Synonyms: adverse; hurtful; inimical; injurious

PEJORATIVE

adj (peh jaw ruh tihv)

DELINEATION

noun (dih lihn ee <u>ay</u> shuhn)

uninspired, boring academic

The speaker's tedious commentary on the subject soon gained him a reputation as a *pedant*.

Synonyms: pedagogue; scholar; schoolmaster

depiction, representation

Mrs. Baxter was very satisfied with the artist's *delineation* of her new house.

Synonyms: figuration; illustration; picture; portraiture

PEDANT

noun (peh daant)

DELUGE

verb (dehl yooj) (dehl yoozh) (day looj) (day loozh) (dih looj) (dih loozh)

teacher

The beloved professor was known as an influential *pedagogue* at the university.

Synonym: instructor

to submerge, overwhelm; to flood

The popular actor was *deluged* with fan mail.

Synonyms: engulf; immerse; inundate; swamp; whelm

PEDAGOGUE

noun (pehd uh gahg)

DEMUR

verb (dih <u>muhr</u>)

KAPLAN

minor sin or offense

Gabriel tends to harp on his brother's *peccadilloes* and never lets him live them down.

Synonyms: failing; fault; lapse; misstep

to express doubts or objections

> When scientific authorities claimed that all the planets revolved around the Earth, Galileo, with his superior understanding of the situation, was forced to *demur*.

Synonyms: expostulate; dissent; protest; remonstrate

PECCADILLO

noun (pehk uh dih loh)

DENIGRATE

verb (<u>deh</u> nih grayt)

scarcity, lack

Because of the relative *paucity* of bananas in the country, their price was very high.

Synonyms: dearth; deficiency; shortage

to slur someone's reputation

> The people still loved the president, despite his enemies' attempts to *denigrate* his character.

Synonyms: belittle; disparage; malign; slander; vilify

PAUCITY

noun (paw suh tee)

DEPOSE

verb (dih <u>pohs</u>)

piece of literature or music imitating other works

The playwright's clever *pastiche* of the well-known fairy tale had the audience rolling in the aisles.

Synonyms: medley; spoof

to remove from a high position, as from a throne

After he was *deposed* from his throne, the king spent the rest of his life in exile.

Synonyms: dethrone; displace; overthrow; topple; unseat

PASTICHE

noun (pah steesh)

KAPLAN

DEPRAVITY

noun (dih praav ih tee)

---

stinginess

Ethel gained a reputation for *parsimony* when she refused to pay for her daughter's college education.

Synonyms: economy; frugality; meanness; miserliness

sinfulness, moral corruption

The *depravity* of the actor's Hollywood lifestyle shocked his traditional parents.

Synonyms: corruption; debauchery; decadence; degradation; enormity

PARSIMONY

noun (pahr sih moh nee)

DEPRECATE

verb (dehp rih kayt)

to ward off or deflect

Kari *parried* every question the interviewer fired at her, much to his frustration.

Synonyms: avoid; evade; repel

to belittle; to disparage

> Ernest *deprecated* his own contribution, instead praising the efforts of his coworkers.

Synonyms: denigrate; discount; minimize

PARRY

verb (paa ree)

DEPRECIATE

verb (dih pree shee ayt)

of limited scope or outlook, provincial

It was obvious that Victor's *parochial* mentality would clash with Ivonne's liberal open-mindedness.

Synonyms: insular; narrow; restricted

to lose value gradually

> The Barrettas sold their house, fearful that its value would *depreciate* due to the nuclear reactor being built around the corner.

Synonym: lessen

PAROCHIAL

adj (puh ro kee uhl)

DEROGATE

verb (dehr uh gayt)

discussion, usually between enemies

The peace organization tried in vain to schedule a *parley* between the warring countries.

Synonyms: confabulation; conference

to belittle; to disparage

The sarcastic old man never stopped *derogating* the efforts of his daughter, even after she won the Nobel Prize.

Synonym: detract

PARLEY

noun (pahr lee)

DESECRATE

verb (<u>dehs</u> ih krayt)

equality

Mrs. Lutskaya tried to maintain *parity* between her children, although each claimed she gave the other preferential treatment.

Synonyms: equivalence; evenness; par

to abuse something sacred

> The archaeologist tried to explain to the explorer that he had *desecrated* the temple by spitting in it.

Synonyms: defile; degrade; profane; violate

PARITY

noun (paa ruh tee)

DESICCATE

verb (<u>deh</u> sih kayt)

impressive array

Corrina sifted through a *panoply* of job offers before finally deciding on one.

Synonym: large variety

to dry completely, dehydrate

> The hot desert sun will *desiccate* anyone who dares spend the day there without a source of water.

Synonyms: evaporate; exsiccate; parch

PANOPLY

noun (pān uh plee)

DESPONDENT

adj (dih spahn duhnt)

cure-all

Some claim that vitamin C is a *panacea* for all sorts of illnesses, but I have my doubts.

Synonyms: elixir; miracle drug; sovereign remedy

discouraged, dejected

Mr. Baker was lonely and *despondent* after his wife's death.

Synonyms: depressed; desolate; forlorn; sad

PANACEA

noun (paan uh see uh)

DESPOT

noun (dehs puht) (dehs paht)

to make less serious, ease

The accused's crime was so vicious that the defense lawyer could not *palliate* it for the jury.

Synonyms: alleviate; assuage; extenuate; mitigate

tyrannical ruler

The *despot* banished half the nobles in his court on a whim.

Synonyms: authoritarian; autocrat; dictator; totalitarian

PALLIATE

verb (paa lee ayt)

DESTITUTE

adj (dehs tih toot) (dehs tih tyoot)

to lose strength or interest

Over time, the model's beauty *palled*, though her haughty attitude remained intact.

Synonyms: tire; weary

very poor, poverty-stricken

After the stock market crash, Jeanette was *destitute*, forced to beg on the streets in order to survive.

Synonyms: broke; impecunious; insolvent; needy; penurious

PALL

verb (pawl)

DESULTORY

adj (dehs uhl tohr ee) (dehz uhl tohr ee)

covering that darkens or obscures; coffin

A *pall* fell over the landscape as the clouds obscured the moon in the night sky.

Synonym: obscurity

at random, rambling, unmethodical

Diane had a *desultory* academic record; she had changed majors 12 times in three years.

Synonym: chaotic

PALL

noun (pawl)

DEXTEROUS

adj (<u>dehk</u> stuhr uhs) (<u>dehk</u> struhs)

idle talk

The journalist eagerly recorded the *palaver* among the football players in the locker room.

Synonym: chit-chat

skilled physically or mentally

The gymnast who won the contest was far more *dexterous* than the other competitors.

Synonyms: adept; adroit; deft; nimble; skilled

PALAVER

noun (puh laav uhr) (puh lah vuhr)

showy

The billionaire's 200-room palace was considered to be an *ostentatious* display of wealth.

Synonyms: flamboyant; fulsome; gaudy; ornate; pretentious

DIABOLICAL

adj (die uh bahl ih kuhl)

fiendish, wicked

Sherlock Holmes's archenemy is the *diabolical* Professor Moriarty.

Synonym: evil

OSTENTATIOUS

adj (ah stehn tay shuhs)

DIAPHANOUS

adj (die aaf uh nuhs)

apparent

The *ostensible* reason for his visit was to borrow a book, but secretly he wanted to chat with Wanda.

Synonyms: represented; supposed; surface

allowing light to show through; delicate

> Ginny's *diaphanous* gown failed to disguise the fact that she was wearing ripped panty hose.

Synonyms: gauzy; tenuous; translucent; transparent; sheer

OSTENSIBLE

adj (ah stehn sih buhl)

DIATRIBE

noun (<u>die</u> uh trieb)

wealth

Livingston considered his expensive car to be a symbol of *opulence.*

Synonyms: affluence; luxury; prosperity

bitter verbal attack

> During the CEO's lengthy *diatribe*, the board members managed to remain calm and self-controlled.

Synonyms: fulmination; harangue; jeremiad; philippic; tirade

OPULENCE

noun (ah pyoo lehns)

DICHOTOMY

noun (die <u>kah</u> tuh mee)

burdensome

The assignment was so difficult to manage that it proved *onerous* to the team in charge of it.

Synonyms: arduous; demanding; exacting; oppressive; rigorous

division into two parts

Westerns often feature a simple *dichotomy* between good guys and bad guys.

Synonyms: bifurcation; distinction; opposition; split

ONEROUS

adj (ōh neh ruhs)

DICTUM

noun (<u>dihk</u> tuhm)

having infinite knowledge, all-seeing

Fiction writers have the ability to be *omniscient* about the characters they create.

Synonym: all-knowing

authoritative statement; popular saying

Chris tried to live his life in accordance with the *dictum* “Two wrongs don’t make a right.”

Synonyms: adage; aphorism; apothegm; decree; edict

OMNISCIENT

adj (ahm nih shehnt)

DIDACTIC

adj (die <u>daak</u> tihk)

too helpful, meddlesome

The *officious* waiter butted into the couple's conversation, advising them on how to take out a mortgage.

Synonyms: eager; intrusive; unwanted

excessively instructive

> The father was overly *didactic* with his children, turning every activity into a lesson.

Synonyms: educational; improving; moralistic

OFFICIOUS

adj (uh fihsh uhs)

DIFFIDENCE

noun (dih fih duhns) (dih fih dehns)

to shut; to block

A shadow is thrown across the Earth's surface during a solar eclipse, when the light from the sun is *occluded* by the moon.

Synonyms: close; obstruct

shyness, lack of confidence

Steve's *diffidence* during the job interview stemmed from his nervous nature and lack of experience.

Synonyms: reticence; timidity

OCCLUDE

verb (uh klood)

DILATORY

adj (dihl uh tohr ee)

to make unnecessary; to anticipate and prevent

The river was shallow enough for the riders to wade across, which *obviated* the need for a bridge.

Synonyms: avert; deter; forestall; preclude

slow, tending to delay

The congressman used *dilatory* measures to delay the passage of the bill.

Synonyms: sluggish; tardy; unhurried

KAPLAN

OBVIATE

verb (ahb vee ayt)

DIMINUTIVE

adj (dih mihn yuh tihv)

insensitive, stupid, dull, unclear

The directions were so *obtuse* that Alfred did not understand what was expected of him.

Synonyms: blunt; dense; slow

small

Napoleon made up for his *diminutive* stature with his aggressive personality.

Synonyms: minscule; short; tiny; wee

OBTUSE

adj (uhb toos)

DISCONCERTING

adj (dihs kuhn suhr tihng)

troublesome, boisterous, unruly

The *obstreperous* toddler, who was always breaking things, was the terror of his nursery school.

Synonym: vociferous

bewildering, perplexing, slightly disturbing

Brad found his mother-in-law's hostile manner so *disconcerting* that he acted like a fool in her presence.

Synonym: upsetting

OBSTREPEROUS

adj (ahb strehp uhr uhs) (uhb strehp uhr uhs)

DISCORDANT

adj (dihs <u>kohr</u> duhnt)

overly submissive, brownnosing

The *obsequious* new employee complimented her supervisor's tie and agreed with him on every issue.

Synonyms: compliant; fawning; groveling; servile; unctuous

disagreeing; at variance

The feelings about the child's education were becoming more and more *discordant*.

Synonyms: cacophonous; dissonant; inharmonious

OBSEQUIOUS

adj (uhb see kwee uhs)

DISCURSIVE

adj (dihs <u>kuhr</u> sihv)

indirect, evasive, misleading, devious

Usually open and friendly, Veronica has been behaving in a curiously *oblique* manner lately.

Synonyms: glancing; slanted; tangential

wandering from topic to topic

> The professor, known for his *discursive* speaking style, covered everything from armadillos to zebras in his zoology lecture.

Synonym: rambling

OBLIQUE

adj (oh bleek)

DISPARAGE

verb (dih spaar ihj)

to make legally invalid; to counteract the effect of

Crystal *nullified* her contract with her publisher when she received a better offer from another company.

Synonyms: cancel; negate; neutralize; undo

to belittle, speak disrespectfully about

> Gregorio loved to *disparage* his brother's dancing skills, pointing out every mistake he made on the floor.

Synonyms: denigrate; deride; derogate; ridicule

NULLIFY

verb (nuh lih fie)

DISSEMBLE

verb (dihs sehm buhl)

shade of meaning

The scholars argued for hours over tiny *nuances* in the interpretation of the last line of the poem.

Synonyms: gradation; subtlety; tone

to pretend; to disguise one's motives

> The villain could *dissemble* to the lawyers no longer—he finally had to confess to the forgery.

Synonyms: camouflage; cloak; conceal; feign

NUANCE

noun (noo ahns)

DISSEMINATE

verb (dih sehm uh nayt)

harmful, unwholesome

The people near the bus covered their noses and mouths to avoid breathing in the *noxious* exhaust fumes.

Synonyms: corrupting; poisonous; toxic; unhealthy

to spread far and wide

> The wire service *disseminates* information so rapidly that events get reported shortly after they happen.

Snonyms: circulate; diffuse; disperse

NOXIOUS

adj (nahk shuhs)

KAPLAN

DISSENSION

noun (dih sehn shunhn)

unfavorable fame

Wayne realized from the silence that greeted him as he entered the office that his *notoriety* preceded him.

Synonyms: disgrace; dishonor; disrepute; infamy; opprobrium

difference of opinion

> The government was forced to abandon the extensive reforms it had planned, due to continued *dissension* within its party ranks about the form these changes should take.

Synonym: disagreement

NOTORIETY

noun (noh tohr ī eh tee)

DISSIPATE

verb (<u>dihs</u> uh payt)

stinking, putrid

A dead mouse trapped in your walls produces a *noisome* odor.

Synonyms: disgusting; foul; malodorous

to scatter; to pursue pleasure to excess

The fog gradually *dissipated*, revealing all the ships docked in the harbor.

Synonyms: carouse; consume; disperse; dissolve; squander

NOISOME

adj (noy suhm)

DISTEND

verb (dih stehnd)

to irritate

I don't particularly like having blue hair—I just do it to *nettle* my parents.

Synonyms: annoy; vex

to swell, inflate, bloat

Her stomach *distended* after she gorged on the six-course meal.

Synonyms: broaden; bulge

NETTLE

verb ($\overline{\text{neh}}$ tuhl)

DITHER

verb (<u>dihth</u> uhr)

novice, beginner

A relative *neophyte* at bowling, Seth rolled all of his balls into the gutter.

Synonyms: apprentice; greenhorn; tyro

to move or act confusedly or without clear purpose

Ellen *dithered* around her apartment, uncertain how to tackle the family crisis.

Synonyms: falter; hesitate; vacillate; waffle; waver

NEOPHYTE

noun (nee oh fiet)

DIURNAL

adj (die <u>uhr</u> nuhl)

not worth considering

It's obvious from our *negligible* dropout rate that our students love our program.

Synonyms: insignificant; nugatory; trifling; trivial

daily

Diurnal creatures tend to become inactive during the night.

Synonyms: daylight; daytime

NEGLIGIBLE

adj (nehg lih jih buhl)

DIVINE

verb (dih <u>vien</u>)

starting to develop, coming into existence

The advertising campaign was still in a *nascent* stage; nothing had been finalized yet.

Synonyms: embryonic; emerging; inchoate; incipient

to foretell or know by inspiration

> The fortune-teller *divined* from the pattern of the tea leaves that her customer would marry five times.

Synonyms: auger; foresee; intuit; predict; presage

KAPLAN

NASCENT

adj (nay sehnt)

DIVISIVE

adj (dih vie sihv) (dih vih sihv) (dih vih zihv)

lowest point

As Lou waited in line to audition for the diaper commercial, he realized he had reached the *nadir* of his acting career.

Synonyms: bottom; depth; pit

creating disunity or conflict

The leader used *divisive* tactics to pit his enemies against each other.

Synonyms: controversial; disruptive; sensitive

NADIR

noun (nay dihr)

DOGMATIC

adj (dahg maat ihk) (dawg maat ihk)

generous

The *munificent* millionaire donated ten million dollars to the hospital.

Synonyms: bountiful; liberal

rigidly fixed in opinion, opinionated

The dictator was *dogmatic*—he, and only he, was right.

Synonyms: authoritative; doctrinaire; inflexible; obstinate

MUNIFICENT

adj (myoo nihf ih suhnt)

diverse

Ken opened the hotel room window, letting in the *multifarious* noises of the great city.

Synonym: various

DOLEFUL

adj (<u>dohl</u> fuhl)

sad, mournful

Looking into the *doleful* eyes of the lonely pony, the girl decided to take him home with her.

Synonyms: dejected; woeful

MULTIFARIOUS

adj (muhl tuh faar ee uhs)

DROLL

adj (drohl)

to mark with spots

Food stains *mottled* the tablecloth.

Synonym: spot

amusing in a wry, subtle way

Although the play couldn't be described as hilarious, it was certainly *droll*.

Synonyms: comic; entertaining; funny; risible; witty

MOTTLE

verb (maht l)

DULCET

adj (duhl suht)

dying, decaying

Thanks to the feminist movement, many sexist customs are now *moribund* in this society.

Synonyms: deceasing; succumbing

pleasant sounding, soothing to the ear

The *dulcet* tone of her voice lulled me to sleep.

Synonyms: agreeable; harmonious; melodious; sweet

MORIBUND

adj (mohr uh buhnd)

DURESS

noun (duhr ehs)

frivolity, gaiety, laughter

Vera's hilarious jokes contributed to the general *mirth* at the dinner party.

Synonyms: glee; hilarity; jollity; merriment

threat of force or intimidation

Under *duress*, the political dissident revealed the names of others in her organization to the secret police.

Synonyms: coercion; compulsion; constraint; pressure

MIRTH

noun (muhrth)

DYSPEPTIC

adj (dihs pehp tihk)

to operate against, work against

The unprofessional employee *militated* against his supervisor, without realizing the ramifications of his actions.

Synonyms: affect; change; influence

gloomy and irritable; suffering from indigestion

The *dyspeptic* young man cast a gloom over the party the minute he walked in.

Synonyms: melancholy; morose; solemn; sour

MILITATE

verb (mihl ih tayt)

EBB

verb (ehb)

courageousness; endurance

The helicopter pilot showed her *mettle* as she landed in the battlefield to rescue the wounded soldiers.

Synonyms: character; fortitude; spirit

to fade away; to recede

From her beachside cottage, Melissa enjoyed watching the tide *ebb* and flow.

Synonyms: abate; retreat; subside; wane; withdraw

METTLE

noun (meht l)

EBULLIENT

adj (ih byool yuhnt) (ih buhl yuhnt)

extremely careful, fastidious, painstaking

To clean every square inch of the huge mural, the restorers had to be *meticulous.*

Synonyms: finicky; fussy; precise; punctilious; scrupulous

exhilarated, full of enthusiasm and high spirits

The *ebullient* child exhausted the baby-sitter, who lacked the energy to keep up with her.

Synonyms: ardent; avid; bubbly; zestful

METICULOUS

adj (mih tihk yuh luhs)

quick, shrewd, unpredictable

Her *mercurial* personality made it difficult to guess how she would react to the bad news.

Synonyms: clever; crafty; volatile; whimsical

EDICT

noun (<u>ee</u> dihkt)

law, command, official public order

Pedestrians often disobey the *edict* that they should not jaywalk.

Synonyms: decree; dictum; directive; fiat; ukase

MERCURIAL

adj (muhr kyoor ee uhl)

EDIFY

verb (<u>eh</u> duh fie)

beggar

"Please, sir, can you spare a dime?" begged the *mendicant* as the businessman walked past.

Synonyms: panhandler; pauper

to instruct morally and spiritually

The guru was paid to *edify* the actress in the ways of Buddhism.

Synonyms: educate; enlighten; guide; teach

MENDICANT

noun (mehn dih kuhnt)

EFFACE

verb (ih <u>fays</u>) (eh <u>fays</u>)

dishonest

So many of her stories were *mendacious* that I decided she must be a pathological liar.

Synonyms: deceitful; false; lying; untruthful

to erase or make illegible

> Benjamin attempted to *efface* all traces of his troubled past by assuming a completely new identity.

Synonyms: expunge; obliterate

MENDACIOUS

adj (mehn day shuhs)

EFFICACIOUS

adj (eff uh <u>kay</u> shuhs)

overly sentimental

The mother's death should have been a touching scene, but the movie's treatment of it was so *maudlin* that, instead of making the audience cry, it made them cringe.

Synonyms: mawkish; saccharine; weepy

effective, efficient

Penicillin was one of the most *efficacious* drugs on the market when it was first introduced; the drug completely eliminated almost all bacterial infections for which it was administered.

Synonyms: effectual; potent

MAUDLIN

adj (mawd lihn)

EFFIGY

noun (<u>eh</u> fuh jee)

to enroll as a member of a college or university

When Suda-May *matriculates* at Yale University this coming fall, she will move to New Haven.

Synonyms: enlist; join

stuffed doll; likeness of a person

The anti-American militants burned Uncle Sam in *effigy* during their demonstration.

Synonyms: dummy; figure; image

MATRICULATE

verb (muh trihk yuh layt)

EFFRONTERY

noun (ih <u>fruhnt</u> uhr ee) (eh <u>fruhnt</u> uhr ee)

strict disciplinarian, one who rigidly follows rules

A complete *martinet*, the official insisted that Pete fill out all the forms again even though he was already familiar with his case.

Synonyms: dictator; stickler; tyrant

impudent boldness; audacity

The receptionist had the *effrontery* to laugh out loud when her boss tripped over a computer wire and fell flat on his face.

Synonyms: brashness; gall; nerve; presumption; temerity

MARTINET

noun (mahr tihn eht)

EFFULGENT

adj (ih fool juhnt) (ih fuhl juhnt)

to evade responsibility by pretending to be ill

A common way to dodge the draft was by *malingering*—faking an illness so as to avoid having to serve in the Army.

Synonyms: fake; shirk

brilliantly shining

The *effulgent* stars that filled the dark evening sky dazzled the sharecroppers.

Synonym: glowing

MALINGER

verb (muh ling guhr)

EFFUSIVE

adj (ih fyoo sihv) (eh fyoo sihv) (eh fyoo zihv)

clumsy, tactless

His *maladroit* comments about the host's poor cooking skills were viewed as inexcusable by the other guests.

Synonyms: awkward; gauche; inept; ungainly

expressing emotion without restraint

The teacher's praise for Brian's brilliant essays was *effusive.*

Synonyms: gushy; overflowing; profuse

MALADROIT

adj (mal uh droyt)

EGREGIOUS

adj (ih gree juhs)

generous, noble in spirit

Although at first he seemed mean, Uncle Frank turned out to be a very *magnanimous* fellow.

Synonyms: forgiving; unselfish

conspicuously bad

> The English textbook contained several *egregious* errors; for example, "grammar" was misspelled as "gramer" throughout.

Synonyms: blatant; flagrant; glaring; gross; rank

MAGNANIMOUS

adj (maag naan uh muhs)

EGRESS

noun (ee grehs)

turmoil; agitated state of mind; whirlpool

The transportation system of the city had collapsed in the *maelstrom* of war.

Synonyms: eddy; turbulence

exit

Commuter trains should have points of convenient *egress* so that during rush hour, passengers can leave the train easily.

Synonym: outlet

MAELSTROM

noun (mayl struhm)

ELUCIDATE

verb (ih loo suh dayt)

plot or scheme

Tired of his employees' endless *machinations* to destroy the company, the boss had them fired.

Synonyms: cabal; conspiracy; design; intrigue

to explain, clarify

> The teacher *elucidated* the reasons why she had failed the student to his upset parents.

Synonyms: define; explicate; illuminate; interpret

MACHINATION

noun (mahk uh nay shuhn)

ENDEMIC

adj (ehn deh mihk)

KAPLAN

sorrowful, mournful; dismal

Marla shed a tear at the *lugubrious* funeral services.

Synonyms: funereal; gloomy; melancholy; somber; woeful

belonging to a particular area; inherent

> The health department determined that the outbreak was *endemic* to the small village, so they quarantined the inhabitants before the virus could spread.

Synonyms: indigenous; local; native

LUGUBRIOUS

adj (loo goo bree uhs)

ENERVATE

verb (<u>ehn</u> uhr vayt)

easily flexed, limber, agile

The *lissome* yoga instructor twisted herself into shapes that her students could only dream of.

Synonyms: graceful; lithe; supple

to weaken, sap strength from

> The guerrillas hoped that a series of surprise attacks would *enervate* the regular army.

Synonyms: debilitate; deplete; drain; exhaust

LISSOME

adj (lihs uhm)

ENGENDER

verb (ehn gehn duhr)

to treat as a celebrity

After the success of his novel, the author was *lionized* by the press.

Synonyms: feast; honor; ply; regale

to produce, cause, bring about

Witnessing the patriotic speech *engendered* Tom's national pride.

Synonyms: generate; procreate; propagate

LIONIZE

verb (li̅e̅ uhn iez)

ENMITY

noun (ehn muh tee)

clear, transparent

Shelley could see all the way to the bottom through the pond's *limpid* water.

Synonyms: lucid; pellucid

hostility, antagonism, ill will

Despite the fact that no one remembered the offense, the *enmity* between the families continued for hundreds of years.

Synonyms: animosity; animus; antipathy; rancor

LIMPID

adj (lim pihd)

ENNUI

noun (ahn <u>wee</u>) (<u>ahn</u> wee)

trickery

The magician was skilled in the arts of *legerdemain*.

Synonym: adroitness

boredom, lack of interest and energy

> Joe tried to alleviate the *ennui* he felt while doing his tedious job by shopping online.

Synonyms: listlessness; tedium; world-weariness

LEGERDEMAIN

noun (lehj uhr duh mayn)

ENSCONCE

verb (ehn skahns)

lethargy, sluggishness

The defeated French army plunged into a state of depressed *lassitude* as they trudged home from Russia.

Synonyms: listlessness; stupor; torpor; weariness

to settle comfortably into a place

> Wayne sold the big, old family house and *ensconced* his aged mother in a cozy little cottage.

Synonym: settle

LASSITUDE

noun (laas ih tood)

ENTREAT

verb (ehn <u>treet</u>)

dawdler, loafer, lazy person

The manager hesitated to fire Biff, his incompetent *laggard* of an assistant, because Biff was the CEO's son.

Synonym: slowpoke

to plead, beg

I *entreated* him to just tell me what the problem was instead of bottling it up inside, but he refused.

Synonyms: beseech; implore; importune; petition; request

LAGGARD

noun (laag uhrd)

EPHEMERAL

adj (ih fehm uhr uhl)

using few words

She was a *laconic* poet who built her reputation on using words as sparingly as possible.

Synonyms: concise; pithy; succinct; terse

momentary, transient, fleeting

> The lives of mayflies seem *ephemeral* to us, since the flies' average life span is a matter of hours.

Synonyms: evanescent; fugitive; momentary; transitory

LACONIC

adj (luh kah nihk)

EPICURE

noun (<u>eh</u> pih kyoor) (<u>eh</u> pih kyuhr)

tearful

Heather always became *lachrymose* when it was time to bid her daughter good-bye.

Synonyms: teary; weepy

a person with refined taste in cuisine

Restaurant critics should be *epicures*, as people rely on their judgments in choosing where to eat.

Synonyms: connoisseur; gastronome; gourmand; gourmet

LACHRYMOSE

adj (laak ruh mohs)

EPIGRAM

noun (eh puh graam)

sound of a funeral bell; omen of death or failure

When the townspeople heard the *knell* from the church belfry, they knew that their mayor had died.

Synonyms: chime; peal; toll

short, witty saying or poem

The poet was renowned for his skill in making up amusing *epigrams*.

Synonyms: adage; aphorism; maxim; saw

KNELL

noun (nehl)

EQUANIMITY

noun (ee kwuh nihm ih tee) (ehk wuh nihm ih tee)

side-by-side placement

The porcelain dog was placed in *juxtaposition* with the straw doghouse on the mantelpiece.

Synonyms: comparison; contrast

calmness, composure

Kelly took the news that she had been fired with outward *equanimity*, though she was crying inside.

Synonyms: aplomb; coolness; poise; sang-froid; serenity

JUXTAPOSITION

noun (juk stuh puh zihsh uhn)

ERUDITE

adj (ehr yuh diet) (ehr uh diet)

philosophy of law

An expert in *jurisprudence*, the esteemed lawyer was often consulted by his colleagues.

Synonym: legal matters

learned, scholarly

The annual meeting of professors brought together the most *erudite* individuals in the field.

Synonyms: cultured; educated; knowledgeable; literate; well-read

JURISPRUDENCE

noun (joor his prood ns)

ESOTERIC

adj (eh suh tehr ihk)

huge force destroying everything in its path

The *juggernaut* of the army surged ahead until it was halted in its tracks by the brutal winter.

Synonym: overwhelming force

understood by only a learned few

> Only a handful of experts are knowledgeable about the *esoteric* world of particle physics.

Synonyms: arcane; mysterious; occult; recondite; secret

JUGGERNAUT

noun (juhg uhr naht)

ETHEREAL

adj (ih <u>theer</u> ee uhl)

belligerent support of one's country

The president's *jingoism* made him declare war on other countries at the slightest provocation.

Synonyms: nationalism

not earthly, spiritual; delicate

Her delicate, *ethereal* beauty made her a popular model for pre-Raphaelite artists.

Synonyms: airy; diaphanous; gossamer; intangible; sheer

JINGOISM

noun (jing goh ihz uhm)

envious; obnoxious

It is cruel and *invidious* for parents to play favorites with their children.

Synonyms: discriminatory; insulting; jaundiced; resentful

ETHOS

noun (ee thohs)

belief or character of a group

> In accordance with the *ethos* of his people, the man completed the tasks that would allow him to become the new chief.

Synonym: sentiment

INVIDIOUS

adj (ihn vihd ee uhs)

EVANESCENT

adj (eh vuh nehs uhnt)

verbal abuse

A stream of *invectives* poured from Mrs. Pratt's mouth as she watched the vandals smash her ceramic frog.

Synonyms: denunciation; revilement; vituperation

momentary, transitory, short-lived

> It is lucky that solar eclipses are *evanescent*, or the world would never see sunlight.

Synonyms: ephemeral; fleeting; fugitive; transient

INVECTIVE

noun (ihn vehk tihv)

EVINCE

verb (ih <u>vihns</u>)

to harden; to accustom; to become used to

Eventually, Hassad became *inured* to the sirens that went off every night and could sleep through them.

Synonyms: condition; familiarize; habituate

to show clearly, display, signify

The new secretary *evinced* impressive typing and filing skills.

Synonym: demonstrate

INURE

verb (ihn yoor)

EXACERBATE

verb (ihg <u>zaas</u> uhr bayt)

uncompromising, refusing to be reconciled

The professor was *intransigent* on the deadline, insisting that everyone turn the assignment in on Friday.

Synonyms: obstinate; unyielding

to aggravate; to intensify the bad qualities of

> It is unwise to take aspirin to relieve heartburn; instead of providing relief, the drug will only *exacerbate* the problem.

Synonyms: deepen; escalate; worsen

INTRANSIGENT

adj (ihn traan suh juhnt) (ihn traan zuh juhnt)

EXCULPATE

verb (<u>ehk</u> skuhl payt) (ihk <u>skuhl</u> payt)

to insert; to intervene

The policeman *interposed* himself between the two men who were about to start fighting.

Synonym: interfere

to clear of blame or fault, vindicate

> The legal system is intended to convict those who are guilty and to *exculpate* those who are innocent.

Synonyms: acquit; exonerate

INTERPOSE

verb (ihn tuhr pohz)

to insert; to change by adding new words or material

The editor *interpolated* a few new sentences into the manuscript, and the new edition was ready to print.

Synonym: intercalate

EXECRABLE

adj (ehk sih kruh buhl)

utterly detestable, abhorrent

The stew tasted *execrable* after the cook accidentally dumped a pound of salt into it.

Synonyms: awful; hateful; horrible; inferior; terrible

INTERPOLATE

verb (ihn tuhr puh layt)

EXHORT

verb (ihg zohrt)

trespasser; meddler in others' affairs

The wolf pack rejected the lone pup as an *interloper*.

Synonym: intruder

to urge or incite by strong appeals

> Rob's friends *exhorted* him to beware of ice on the roads when he insisted on driving home in the middle of a snowstorm.

Synonyms: convince; inspire; press; prod; provoke

INTERLOPER

noun (ihn tuhr loh puhr)

EXHUME

verb (ihg <u>zoom</u>) (ihg <u>zyoom</u>) (ihk <u>syoom</u>) (ehks <u>hyoom</u>)

to forbid, prohibit

The matron *interdicted* male visits to the girls' dorm rooms after midnight.

Synonyms: ban; outlaw

to remove from a grave; uncover a secret

The archaeologist *exhumed* the scrolls from the ancient tomb.

Synonyms: disinter; unearth

INTERDICT

verb (ihn tuhr dihkt)

EXIGENT

adj (ehk suh juhnt)

sly, treacherous, devious

Iago's *insidious* comments about Desdemona fuelled Othello's feelings of jealousy regarding his wife.

Synonyms: alluring; deceitful; perfidious

urgent; excessively demanding

> The tank was losing gasoline so rapidly that it was *exigent* to stop the source of the leak.

Synonyms: compelling; critical; crucial; imperative; pressing

INSIDIOUS

adj (ihn sihd ee uhs)

EXONERATE

verb (ihg <u>zahn</u> uh rayt)

sin, evil act

The principal believed that the *iniquity* the student committed was grounds for expulsion.

Synonyms: immorality; injustice; vice; wickedness

to clear of blame, absolve

The fugitive was *exonerated* when another criminal confessed to committing the crime.

Synonyms: acquit; exculpate; vindicate

INIQUITY

noun (ih nihk wih tee)

EXPEDIENT

adj (ihk <u>spee</u> dee uhnt)

hostile, unfriendly

Even though a cease-fire had been in place for months, the two sides were still *inimical* to each other.

Synonyms: adverse; antagonistic; harmful; injurious

convenient, efficient, practical

It was considered more *expedient* to send the fruit directly to the retailer instead of through a middleman.

Synonyms: appropriate; sensible; useful

INIMICAL

adj (ih nihm ih kuhl)

EXPIATE

verb (<u>ehk</u> spee ayt)

entrance

Ed hoped that the mailroom job would provide him with an *ingress* into the company.

Synonym: entry

to atone; to make amends

> The nun *expiated* her sins by scrubbing the floor of the convent on her hands and knees.

Synonyms: compensate; pay

INGRESS

noun (ihn grehs)

EXPURGATE

verb (ehk spuhr gayt)

straightforward, open; naïve and unsophisticated

She was so *ingenuous* that her friends feared that her innocence would be exploited when she visited the big city.

Synonyms: artless; candid; natural; simple; unaffected

to censor

Government propagandists *expurgated* all negative references to the dictator from the film.

Synonyms: bowdlerize; cut; sanitize

INGENUOUS

adj (ihn jehn yoo uhs)

EXTEMPORANEOUS

adj (ihk stehm puh <u>ray</u> nee uhs)

original, clever, inventive

Luther found an *ingenious* way to solve the complex math problem.

Synonyms: cunning; imaginative; shrewd

unrehearsed, on the spur of the moment

> Jan gave an *extemporaneous* performance of a Monty Python skit at her surprise birthday party.

Synonyms: ad-lib; impromptu; spontaneous; unprepared

INGENIOUS

adj (ih jeen yuhs)

EXTRICATE

verb (<u>ehk</u> strih kayt)

inflexible, unyielding

The *inexorable* force of the tornado swept away their house.

Synonyms: adamant; obdurate; relentless

to free from; to disentangle

The fly was unable to *extricate* itself from the flypaper.

Synonyms: disencumber; disengage; release; untangle

INEXORABLE

adj (ihn ehk suhr uh buhl)

FALLOW

adj (<u>faa</u> loh)

unable to move, tending to inactivity

In the heat of the desert afternoon, lizards lie *inert.*

Synonyms: dormant; idle; inactive; lethargic; sluggish

uncultivated, unused

> This field should lie *fallow* for a year so that the soil does not become completely depleted.

Synonyms: idle; inactive; unseeded

INERT

adj (ihn uhrt)

FASTIDIOUS

adj (faa <u>stihd</u> ee uhs) (fuh <u>stihd</u> ee uhs)

unquestionable

His *indubitable* cooking skills made it all the more astonishing when the Thanksgiving dinner he prepared tasted awful.

Synonyms: apparent; certain; unassailable

careful with details

> Brett was normally so *fastidious* that Rachel was astonished to find his desk littered with clutter.

Synonyms: meticulous; painstaking; precise; punctilious; scrupulous

INDUBITABLE

adj (ihn doo bih tuh buhl) (ihn dyoo bih tuh buhl)

FATUOUS

adj (<u>faach</u> oo uhs)

habitually lazy, idle

Her *indolent* ways got her fired from many jobs.

Synonyms: fainéant; languid; lethargic; slothful; sluggish

stupid; foolishly self-satisfied

Ted's *fatuous* comments always embarrassed his keen-witted wife.

Synonyms: absurd; ludicrous; preposterous; ridiculous; silly

INDOLENT

adj (ihn duh luhnt)

FECUND

adj (fee kuhn) (fehk uhnd)

angry, incensed, offended

The innocent passerby was *indignant* when the police treated him as a suspect in the crime.

Synonyms: furious; irate; ireful; mad; wrathful

fertile, fruitful, productive

The *fecund* woman gave birth to a total of twenty children.

Synonyms: flourishing; prolific

INDIGNANT

adj (ihn dihg nuhnt)

FELICITOUS

adj (fih lihs ih tuhs)

very poor

Because the suspect was *indigent*, the state paid for his legal representation.

Synonyms: destitute; impecunious; impoverished; needy; penniless

suitable, appropriate; well spoken

> The father of bride made a *felicitous* speech at the wedding, contributing to the success of the event.

Synonym: fitting

INDIGENT

adj (ihn dih juhnt)

FERVID

adj (fuhr vihd)

never tired

Theresa seemed *indefatigable*, barely sweating after a 10-mile run.

Synonyms: inexhaustible; unflagging; weariless

passionate, intense, zealous

> The fans of Maria Callas were particularly *fervid*, doing anything to catch a glimpse of the great singer.

Synonyms: ardent; avid; eager; enthusiastic; vehement

INDEFATIGABLE

adj (ihn dih faat ih guh buhl)

FETID

adj (<u>feh</u> tihd)

sudden invasion

The army was unable to resist the *incursion* of the rebel forces into their territory.

Synonym: raid

foul-smelling, putrid

The *fetid* stench from the trash heap caused Laura to wrinkle her nose in disgust.

Synonyms: funky; malodorous; noisome; rank; stinky

INCURSION

noun (ihn kuhr zhuhn) (ihn kuhr shuhn)

FETTER

verb (feh tuhr)

to blame, charge with a crime

His suspicious behavior after the break-in led authorities to *inculpate* him.

Synonym: incriminate

to bind, chain, confine

> Lorna *fettered* the bikes together so that it would be less likely that they would be stolen.

Synonyms: curb; handcuff; manacle; shackle; tether

INCULPATE

verb (ihn kuhl payt) (ihn kuhl payt)

FLACCID

adj (<u>flaa</u> sihd)

to teach, impress in the mind

Most parents blithely *inculcate* their children with their political views instead of allowing their children to select their own.

Synonyms: implant; indoctrinate; instill; preach

limp, flabby, weak

> The woman jiggled her *flaccid* arms in disgust, resolving to begin lifting weights as soon as possible.

Synonyms: floppy; soft

INCULCATE

verb (ihn kuhl kayt) (ihn kuhl kayt)

FLORID

adj (flohr ihd) (flahr ihd)

beginning to exist or appear; in an initial stage

At that point, her financial problems were only *incipient* and she could still pay her bills.

Synonyms: basic; developing

gaudy, extremely ornate

The palace had been decorated in an excessively *florid* style; every surface had been carved and gilded.

Synonyms: flamboyant; garish; loud; ornate; ostentatious

INCIPIENT

adj (ihn sihp ee uhnt)

FOIBLE

noun (foy buhl)

KAPLAN

imperfectly formed or formulated

As her thoughts on the subject were still in *inchoate* form, Amalia could not explain what she meant.

Synonyms: formless; undefined

minor weakness or character flaw

Her habit of always arriving late is just a *foible*, although it is somewhat rude.

Synonyms: blemish; failing; fault; frailty; vice

INCHOATE

adj (ihn koh iht)

FOMENT

verb (foh <u>mehnt</u>)

combustible, flammable, burning easily

Gasoline is so *incendiary* that cigarette smoking is forbidden at gas stations.

Synonyms: explosive; inflammable

to arouse or incite

> The protesters tried to *foment* feeling against the war through their speeches and demonstrations.

Synonyms: abet; instigate; promote

INCENDIARY

adj (ihn sehn dee ehr ee)

FORBEARANCE

noun (fohr baar uhns)

to call into question; to attack verbally

"How dare you *impugn* my honorable motives?" protested the lawyer on being accused of ambulance chasing.

Synonyms: challenge; dispute

patience, restraint, leniency

> Collette decided to exercise *forbearance* with her assistant's numerous errors in light of the fact that he was new on the job.

Synonyms: resignation; tolerance

IMPUGN

verb (ihm pyoon)

FORSWEAR

verb (fohr <u>swayr</u>)

without planning or foresight; negligent

The *improvident* woman spent all the money she received in her court settlement within two weeks.

Synonym: unprepared

to repudiate, renounce, disclaim, reject

> I was forced to *forswear* French fries after the doctor told me that my cholesterol was too high.

Synonym: abjure

IMPROVIDENT

adj (ihm prahv ih duhnt)

FORTE

noun (<u>fohr</u> tay)

to ask repeatedly, beg

The assistant *importuned* her boss with constant requests for a raise and promotion.

Synonyms: annoy; trouble

strong point, something a person does well

> Since math was Dan's *forte*, his friends always asked him to calculate the bill whenever they went out to dinner together.

Synonyms: métier; specialty

IMPORTUNE

verb (ihm pohr toon) (ihm pohr chuhn)

FOUNDER

verb (<u>fown</u> duhr)

quick to act without thinking

The *impetuous* day trader rushed to sell his stocks at the first hint of trouble, and lost $300,000.

Synonyms: impulsive; passionate

to sink; to fall helplessly

> After colliding with the jagged rock, the ship *foundered*, forcing the crew to abandon it.

Synonyms: immerse; miscarry; plunge

IMPETUOUS

adj (ihm peh choo uhs) (ihm pehch wuhs)

FRACAS

noun (<u>fraak</u> uhs) (<u>fray</u> kuhs)

impossible to penetrate; incapable of being affected

A good raincoat should be *impervious* to moisture.

Synonyms: callous; immune

noisy dispute

When the players discovered that the other team was cheating, a violent *fracas* ensued.

Synonyms: brawl; broil; donnybrook; fray; melee

IMPERVIOUS

adj (ihm puhr vee uhs)

FRACTIOUS

adj (<u>fraak</u> shuhs)

poor, having no money

After the crash of thousands of tech startups, many Internet millionaires found themselves *impecunious.*

Synonyms: destitute; impoverished; indigent; needy; penniless

unruly, rebellious

> The general had a hard time maintaining discipline among his *fractious* troops.

Synonyms: contentious; cranky; peevish; quarrelsome

IMPECUNIOUS

adj (ihm pih kyoo nyuhs) (ihm pih kyoo nee uhs)

FULSOME

adj (<u>fool</u> suhm)

unchangeable, invariable

Poverty was an *immutable* fact of life for the unfortunate Wood family; every moneymaking scheme they tried failed.

Synonyms: fixed; permanent; stationary; steady

sickeningly excessive; repulsive

> Diana felt nauseous at the sight of the rich, *fulsome* dishes weighing down the table at the banquet.

Synonyms: copious; overdone

IMMUTABLE

adj (ihm myoot uh buhl)

GAMBOL

verb (<u>gaam</u> buhl)

to infuse; to dye, wet, moisten

Marcia struggled to *imbue* her children with decent values, a difficult task in this day and age.

Synonyms: charge; impregnate; permeate; pervade

to dance or skip around playfully

The parents gathered to watch the children *gambol* about the yard.

Synonym: frolic

IMBUE

verb (ihm byoo)

GARNER

verb (<u>gahr</u> nuhr)

type or kind

“I try not to associate with men of his *ilk*,” sniffed the respectable old lady.

Synonyms: character; class; nature; sort; variety

to gather and store

> The director managed to *garner* financial backing from several different sources for her next project.

Synonyms: acquire; amass; glean; harvest; reap

ILK

noun (ihlk)

GARRULOUS

adj (gaar uh luhs) (gaar yuh luhs)

---

disgraceful and dishonorable

He was humiliated by his *ignominious* dismissal.

Synonyms: debasing; degrading; despicable; shameful

very talkative

The *garrulous* parakeet distracted its owner with its continuous talking.

Synonyms: chatty; loquacious; prolix; verbose; voluble

IGNOMINIOUS

adj (ihg nuh mih nee uhs)

GIBE

verb (jieb)

peculiarity of temperament, eccentricity

His numerous *idiosyncrasies* included a fondness for wearing bright green shoes with mauve socks.

Synonyms: humor; oddity; quirk

to make heckling, taunting remarks

> Tina *gibed* at her brothers mercilessly as they clumsily attempted to pitch the tent.

Synonyms: deride; jeer; mock; ridicule; twit

IDIOSYNCRASY

noun (ih dee uh sihn kruh see)

GLIB

adj (glihb)

one who attacks traditional beliefs

His lack of regard for traditional beliefs soon established him as an *iconoclast.*

Synonyms: dissident; nonconformist; rebel

fluent in an insincere manner; offhand, casual

> The slimy politician managed to continue gaining supporters because he was a *glib* speaker.

Synonyms: easy; superficial

ICONOCLAST

noun (ie kahn uh klaast)

GLOWER

verb (glow uhr)

purposeful exaggeration for effect

When the mayor claimed his town was one of the seven wonders of the world, outsiders classified his statement as *hyperbole*.

Synonyms: embellishment; inflation; magnification

to glare, stare angrily and intensely

The cranky waitress *glowered* at the indecisive customer.

Synonyms: frown; scowl

HYPERBOLE

noun (hie puhr boh lee)

very old; whitish or gray from age

The old man's *hoary* beard contrasted starkly to the new stubble of his teenage grandson.

Synonyms: ancient; antediluvian; antique; vernerable; vintage

GOAD

verb (gohd)

to prod or urge

Denise *goaded* her sister Leigh into running the marathon with her.

Synonyms: impel; incite; provoke; rouse; stimulate

HOARY

adj (hohr ee) (haw ree)

KAPLAN

GRATIS

adj (grah tihs) (gray tihs)

wilderness

The anthropologists noticed that the people had moved out of the cities and into the *hinterland.*

Synonyms: backcountry; frontier

free, costing nothing

The college students swarmed around the *gratis* buffet in the lobby.

Synonyms: complimentary; costless

HINTERLAND

noun (hihn tuhr laand)

GUILE

noun (gie uhl)

excessively rigid; dry and stiff

The *hidebound* old patriarch would not tolerate any opposition to his orders.

Synonyms: conservative; inflexible

trickery, deception

> Greg used considerable *guile* to acquire his rent-controlled apartment, even claiming to be a Vietnam vet.

Synonyms: artifice; cunning; duplicity; wiliness

HIDEBOUND

adj (hīed bownd)

GUSTATORY

adj (<u>goos</u> tuh tohr ee)

tightly sealed

The *hermetic* seal of the jar proved impossible to break.

Synonyms: airtight; impervious; watertight

relating to sense of taste

> Murdock claimed that he loved cooking because he enjoyed the *gustatory* pleasures in life.

Synonym: culinary

HERMETIC

adj (huhr meh tihk)

HACKNEYED

adj (haak need)

extremely distressing, terrifying

We stayed up all night listening to Dave and Will talk about their *harrowing* adventures at sea.

Synonyms: tormenting; vexing

worn out by overuse

We always mock my father for his *hackneyed* expressions and dated hairstyle.

Synonyms: banal; shopworn; stale; trite

HARROWING

adj (haa roh ng)

HAPLESS

adj (<u>haap</u> luhs)

precursor, sign of something to come

The groundhog's appearance on February 2 is a *harbinger* of spring.

Synonyms: forerunner; herald; omen; presage

unfortunate, having bad luck

I wish someone would give that poor, *hapless* soul some food and shelter.

Synonyms: ill-fated; ill-starred; jinxed; luckless; unlucky

HARBINGER

noun (haar buhn juhr)

SAT ROOT LIST

A, AN—not, without

AB, A—from, away, apart

AC, ACR—sharp, sour

AD, A—to, towards

ALI, ALTR—another

AM, AMI—love

AMBI, AMPHI—both

AMBL, AMBUL—walk

ANIM—mind, spirit, breath

ANN, ENN—year

ANTE, ANT—before

ANTHROP—human

ANTI, ANT—against, opposite

AUD—hear

AUTO—self

BELLI, BELL—war

BENE, BEN—good

BI—two

BIBLIO—book

BIO—life

BURS—money, purse

CAD, CAS, CID—happen, fall

CAP, CIP—head

CARN—flesh

CAP, CAPT, CEPT, CIP—take, hold, seize

CED, CESS—yield, go

CHROM—color

CHRON—time

CIDE—murder

CIRCUM—around

CLIN, CLIV—slope

CLUD, CLUS, CLAUS, CLOIS—shut, close

CO, COM, CON—with, together

COGN, GNO—know

CONTRA—against

CORP—body

COSMO, COSM—world

CRAC, CRAT—rule, power

CRED—trust, believe

CRESC, CRET—grow

CULP—blame, fault

CURR, CURS—run

DE—down, out, apart

DEC—ten, tenth

DEMO, DEM—people

DI, DIURN—day

DIA—across

DIC, DICT—speak

DIS, DIF, DI—not, apart, away

DOC, DOCT—teach

DOL—pain

DUC, DUCT—lead

EGO—self

EN, EM—in, into

ERR—wander

EU—well, good

EX, E—out, out of

FAC, FIC, FECT, FY, FEA—make, do

FAL, FALS—deceive

FERV—boil

FID—faith, trust

FLU, FLUX—flow

FORE—before

FRAG, FRAC—break

FUS—pour

GEN—birth, class, kin

GRAD, GRESS—step

GRAPH, GRAM—writing

GRAT—pleasing

GRAV, GRIEV—heavy

GREG—crowd, flock

HABIT, HIBIT—have, hold

HAP—by chance

HELIO, HELI—sun

HETERO—other

HOL—whole

HOMO—same

HOMO—man

HYDR—water

HYPER—too much, excess

HYPO—too little, under

IN, IG, IL, IM, IR—not

IN, IL, IM, IR—in, on, into

INTER—between, among

INTRA, INTR—within

IT, ITER—between, among

JECT, JET—throw

JOUR—day

JUD—judge

JUNCT, JUG—join

JUR—swear, law

LAT—side

LAV, LAU, LU—wash

LEG, LEC, LEX—read, speak

LEV—light

LIBER—free

LIG, LECT—choose, gather

LIG, LI, LY—bind

LING, LANG—tongue

LITER—letter

LITH—stone

LOQU, LOC, LOG—speech, thought

LUC, LUM—light

LUD, LUS—play

MACRO—great

MAG, MAJ, MAS, MAX—great

MAL—bad

MAN—hand

MAR—sea

MATER, MATR—mother

MEDI—middle

MEGA—great

MEM, MEN—remember

METER, METR, MENS—measure

MICRO—small

MIS—wrong, bad, hate

MIT, MISS—send

MOLL—soft

MON, MONIT—warn

MONO—one

MOR—custom, manner

MOR, MORT—dead

MORPH—shape

MOV, MOT, MOB, MOM—move

MUT—change

NAT, NASC—born

NAU, NAV—ship, sailor

NEG—not, deny

NEO—new

NIHIL—none, nothing

NOM, NYM—name

NOX, NIC, NEC, NOC—harm

NOV—new

NUMER—number

OB—against

OMNI—all

ONER—burden

OPER—work

PAC—peace

PALP—feel

PAN—all

PATER, PATR—father

PATH, PASS—feel, suffer

PEC—money

PED, POD—foot

PEL, PULS—drive

PEN—almost

PEND, PENS—hang

PER—through, by, for, throughout

PER—against, destruction

PERI—around

PET—seek, go towards

PHIL—love

PHOB—fear

PHON—sound

PLAC—calm, please

PON, POS—put, place

PORT—carry

POT—drink

POT—power

PRE—before

PRIM, PRI—first

PRO—ahead, forth

PROTO—first

PROX, PROP—near

PSEUDO—false

PYR—fire

QUAD, QUAR, QUAT—four

QUES, QUER, QUIS, QUIR—question

QUIE—quiet

QUINT, QUIN—five

RADI, RAMI—branch

RECT, REG—straight, rule

REG—king, rule

RETRO—backward

RID, RIS—laugh

ROG—ask

RUD—rough, crude

RUPT—break

SACR, SANCT—holy

SCRIB, SCRIPT, SCRIV—write

SE—apart, away

SEC, SECT, SEG—cut

SED, SID—sit

SEM—seed, sow

SEN—old

SENT, SENS—feel, think

SEQU, SECU—follow

SIM, SEM—similar, same

SIGN—mark, sign

SIN—curve

SOL—sun

SOL—alone

SOMN—sleep

SON—sound

SOPH—wisdom

SPEC, SPIC—see, look

SPER—hope

SPERS, SPAR—scatter

SPIR—breathe

STRICT, STRING—bind

STRUCT, STRU—build

SUB—under

SUMM—highest

SUPER, SUR—above

SURGE, SURRECT—rise

SYN, SYM—together

TACIT, TIC—silent

TACT, TAG, TANG—touch

TEN, TIN, TAIN—hold, twist

TEND, TENS, TENT—stretch

TERM—end

TERR—earth, land

TEST—witness

THE—god

THERM—heat

TIM—fear, frightened

TOP—place

TORT—twist

TORP—stiff, numb

TOX—poison

TRACT—draw

TRANS—across, over, through, beyond

TREM, TREP—shake

TURB—shake

UMBR—shadow

UNI, UN—one

URB—city

VAC—empty

VAL, VAIL—value, strength

VEN, VENT—come

VER—true

VERB—word

VERT, VERS—turn

VICT, VINC—conquer

VID, VIS—see

VIL—base, mean

VIV, VIT—life

VOC, VOK, VOW—call, voice

VOL—wish

VOLV, VOLUT—turn, roll

VOR—eat